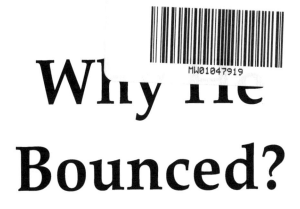

Why He Bounced?

Why men stop calling, texting,
slow down, or simply walk away!

By

Phil Turner Jr.

Philio Publishing, www.philiopublishing.com
Copyright © 2012 by Phil Turner Jr.
www.philturnerjr.com

FIRST EDITION published 2012
ISBN-10: 0962299677

ISBN-13: 978-0-9622996-7-4

Table of Contents

"A man's dating skills do not translate into what type of husband he will be for you."

Disclaimer

The information provided in this book is designed for enlightenment purposes only and is not intended to replace the advice of licensed professionals.

Phil Turner Jr. does not provide guarantees that you will resolve your relationship issues by reading *Why He Bounced*. However, he offers this book as a positive guide to assist you in shifting your consciousness on the relationship issues explored in it.

Introduction

This book is jam-packed with powerful tips and information about why a man will suddenly leave a relationship. I am using a catchy, urban colloquial title: *Why He Bounced?*

In this book, you will learn how to **speak the language of men** and at least have a little more clarity regarding most of their actions in a relationship.

I'm aware that there are tons of relationship books available, and you may be wondering why you should read this book. Well, it has you, the reader, in mind by being to the point and not skimping on the information. This means you will not find love stories with vague hints about the issues. The information provided here is direct.

Additionally, I hate seeing women hurt and want to assist in protecting hearts. You may find some things in this book that may be difficult, but it is only designed to serve you as a father or big brother would.

As I always say, most women are not single by choice. They seek men who are their intellectual equal and with the same values. So why does it seem so difficult to find and keep a man? I believe it has everything to do with skills and attitude.

Men want women to understand them. Even though it appears that men do not have the same problems as women, they have just as many difficulties meeting that special woman. Just for the record: Men get hurt often and have difficulties getting over women who say, "It's not you but me." A man is then left picking up the pieces of his heart and just feeling out of it. He may not want to bathe, may be waddling around in a depressive state, at the bar drinking till he passes out, playing that sad song over and over again, calling his friends for some type of connection, or maybe going to church hoping to feel better. Some men just do other stupid things to deal with relationship hurt.

However I would say that, yes, it is easier for most men to get over a past hurt. This is only because a pool of prepared women is readily available on the market today. I know that sucks to read, or maybe hear, but it's the truth.

I've heard so many women say, "He was a jerk with me and now he is married--just one year after our break-up. Why couldn't he...with me?" This is my question: Was he actually a jerk, or did you expect him to be flawless? Maybe you called mistakes or habits "bad behavior." You see, some women tolerate flaws because they understand that it has nothing to do with how they are actually treated in the relationship. Such a woman will understand that there are some things she may not like about him, just as there are things about her that he may not like. She will know how he wants to be treated. He, in turn, will find this to be a woman he cannot live without; and if in the right stage, he will settle down.

The purpose of this book is to teach you why a man leaves a relationship suddenly.

Women are extremely powerful in a relationship. By using this power, along with solid CIA-style intelligence, you can become the woman he cannot live without. You can do this simply by understanding that everything most men do can be considered positioning just to impress a woman and become her super hero. Once a woman learns how to have an approving spirit towards men, becomes her personal best, while using her "that-a-boy" skills, men will be hovering over her air space searching for a runway to land. Oh, how there will be arrivals, not departures!

So, clear your mind, and while you are reading this book, instead of disagreeing with concepts based on your past relationship experiences, think in terms of possibilities. There is no way around what must be done for a successful relationship: focus on giving instead of on what a man can do for you.

Women who experience the "it's-raining-men paradigm" have a few things in common: They understand the laws of proximity, something I teach in my coaching practice. And they take full responsibility for their own feelings. They have a "Love-all-men" attitude and find good in every man they meet, regardless of physical attraction. They read books like this with an "I'm-seeking-to-polish-my-skills" type of attitude and are never negative about men. Their airspace commands respect while alerting men that it is safe for landing. They are confused when women share their negative experiences and problems finding quality men because this is not their reality.

Guess what? You can be that woman from this point on!

About Me

I am a certified strategic interventionist, marriage educator, and relationship coach. My work involves taking my clients from where they are to where they want to be in their relationship. I specialize in helping successful women attract and keep a man.

As a constant student in this area, I have spent the last ten years of my life devoted to relationship-improvement methods. I've coached hundreds of smart and successful women, providing love lessons and assisting them in understanding men. Even though the study of relationships has been my passion, I've received my degrees in Business which helps in the operations of a coaching practice.

My coaching training includes receiving a Certified Strategic Interventionist and Marriage Educator designation from the Robbins Madanes Center for Strategic Intervention. This is the powerful school of coaching with Anthony (Tony) Robbins and Dr. Cloé Madanes. This program offers ground-breaking strategies incorporating human needs psychology and other high quality disciplines including Ericksonian therapy, strategic family therapy, organizational psychology, neuro-linguistics, psychology of influence, strategic studies, traditions of diplomacy and negotiation, and much more.

I am also a trained NLP Practitioner (Neuro-Linguistic Programming), a Prepare/Enrich Facilitator, and have completed training at the Relationship Coaching Institute and many other coaching, "change agent," and relationship programs.

I started researching men and their relationships informally in the year of 2000 and began writing about it in late 2001-2002 in a promotional online email newsletter distributed to over 100,000 members; the feedback from those articles was simply amazing. I have continued this research throughout the years and am using many of the findings in this book.

I am married to a wonderful woman and am, actually, a newlywed (October 2011) after being divorced for seven years.

Why I can help you?

Well, I've been married before, made mistakes, and recently been out in this new dating climate. Therefore I understand very well where you are right now. Additionally, I simply understand men. How? Duh, I'm a man! But also in the last few years, I've interviewed, questioned and interacted with thousands of men in a "What Men Really Want" group for my research and can provide you with a perspective that maybe you have not considered.

There are a lot of relationship do's and don'ts circulating these days, especially since the success of Steve Harvey's books. Now there are hundreds of blogs and many reality shows on match-making and dating, as well as new books being published every month on understanding men, saving your marriage, and online dating. All of the available relationship information can be overwhelming and contradictory.

What I do know is that there are exceptions to every theory or concept written. Some unconventional methods may work even if they are not supposed to. But look at it this way: a broken clock is always right at least two times a day. Yes, "the exceptions" have worked before; this is why I say it is best to stick with sound principles while being flexible.

Just know that every strategy you read about may not work on that great guy in front of you. However, sometimes a non-traditional approach may be effective on certain guys. This is why I say to be flexible. This is true for all of the tips in this book--being flexible will serve you well. Keep an open mind.

So, what does work? Well, for certain, the ability to be vulnerable along with relationship skills and authenticity work. If you have relationship skills and are authentic in your relationships, then these statements are true about you:

1. You are an individual who understands your core gifts (Not talents, but what you deeply believe in and are passionate about. You may be afraid to speak about it or allow it to show up in your life.)
2. You know that your needs usually change based on where you are in life and that your requirements are based on something deeper than just attractions.
3. You are clear on your values and know your rules.
4. You understand that it is not about finding the right man, but being the right woman.

In other words, you must have a clear picture of who you are and what motivates your choices now. This is more easily said than done. But if you put in the necessary personal work, your chances of meeting and settling down with that great guy is one hundred times better and will happen. On top of this, you will simply have a great life. This is why I believe that everyone needs a relationship coach or mentor to help them discover their needs, relationship readiness level, and values. These love-lesson skills are not readily available and are not taught in school, but they are necessary.

What makes me different from other relationship coaches, experts, or mentors in this relationship industry? Well, I'm not sure. However, when I think about it, three things come to mind.

First, I know that I am a devoted student of the relationship industry and only study or read topics by other students of the industry.

Second, I do not believe in giving quick one-size-fits-all relationship advice, especially on radio shows or forums. I like to ask probing question. To really be effective in a person's life regarding their relationship, you need to truly understand their world and history before providing solutions.

Relationships have become a hot and booming industry, especially the how-to-attract-and-keep-a-man segment. It seems that everyone is writing books and speaking on relationships: from ministers and college professors to engineers, and anyone who believes that their title places them in a position to speak about relationships. I'm extremely happy with the interest and will never be negative about anyone's advice. I appreciate it! However, many are not really students of the industry and, even though they have good intentions and are good people, they are in it because it is another profit center. Most of them usually provide only one-size-fits-all type of advice. I like to call this "retail relationship advice." Most of the time, it does not get to the core of problems. The advice is good generally; but without getting to the core, you don't know all of the facts and could send a person away with a flawed action plan. I just don't believe in doing this.

Third, unlike coaches who act as if they are perfect in their relationships, I'm willing to put on the table that, although I have relationship skills and have coached others, I make relationship mistakes just like other men. For example, not always recognizing my conversation tones, being easily distracted and not listening at times, being a little messy, or not following through as I should. I can sometimes become angry or raise my voice and my skills can appear to go out the window for a brief moment.

This is human nature; no one is perfect in their relational skills one hundred percent of the time. But because of my skills, what I do have is awareness, a very important relationship skill. This is why my outbursts are extremely brief. You see, my awareness always kicks in, alerting me to re-evaluate the issue.

That said; just know that experts do not always have it together. Many are not in a relationship, have been divorced so many times that it's hard to count, or have been married so long that they have forgotten what it is even like to date. It doesn't mean that you shouldn't listen or learn from them; actually I believe you should. They can truly teach you by experience. Just know that this thing called "relationship" is just not as easy as one may imply. A happy relationship requires constant work and daily practice--just like brushing your teeth three times a day.

Because I share some of the experiences and issues my clients have faced, I like hearing other men say the exact same thing as I have observed, before tagging a subject as "How men think" or "from a male's perspective."

Through my research I have discovered that there are certain types of men, and that men think differently according to their relationship pattern, personal experiences and current life stage. However, many agree on several concepts. If women can get a basic understanding of men, it can help in learning how to handle them. In other words, learn how to speak men.

This is the information I am providing in this book to help you understand why he bounced or why he will bounce out of your life.

"Most people repeat or react to or escape from the relationship patterns of their parents. All of their reactions to a relationship are actually still coming from a parental influence, more so than from their true self."

Chapter 1

Getting Started

"Asking questions is great and necessary, but it cannot be excessive or it feels like a job instead of a relationship. Relax and see if you can enjoy his company; watch and listen and feel."

The Meaning of Bounce

Some reading this title may be asking, "What does 'bounce' mean?"

Well in the urban dictionary it means "to leave or exit." Here are some examples I've heard:

I'm bored, so let's bounce!
He just bounced after yelling at his woman.
She just bounced when she became angry.

Some might prefer *Why Did He Leave?* Or maybe, *Why Did He Walk Away?* But it doesn't capture the frustration the women I coach express when their man leaves them and they have no clue why. He's as out of control as a bouncing basketball. That's why I prefer *Why He Bounced?*

Rules of Bouncing

There are times when a woman will rack her brain wondering what is going on with a guy. He could be her long-term mate, boyfriend, or a guy she is seeing with an undefined status.

It is important to be clear about whether a man has bounced to clear his head because of something he experienced and defined as disrespectful, or whether he has completely taken himself out of your life.

In this book there are statements regarding when a man may become detached and bounce. The question is why? What does this mean?

Keep in mind that most guys will bounce emotionally first; and in this case, he is noticeably detached or distant from you. However, it doesn't mean that he is out of your life completely. As I just said, you may be racking your brain wondering what happened because he is not talking.

Here is something to consider. Yes, a man must be mature enough to speak what is on his mind and to express why he is acting angry when you don't have a clue what is wrong. Here is the deal: usually in these cases a man is not comfortable talking about the situation because he is puzzling over how to respond. He's not sure what the right protocol is.

For example, it could be that he saw you taking a second peek at a good-looking guy during an outing. This started his brain to wondering if he is what you want. Or, it could be something you said. Either he is unsure how to feel about it, or it has made him feel that he is not the one for you. Just keep in mind that a man does not like to be puzzled or to have the feeling that he is about to be rejected by a woman of interest. Men want things simple, *is she into me, or not? Can I win with this woman, or not? Is she second-guessing or competing with me? Do I want to get into a conversation that makes me uncomfortable or makes me look weak?*

Men have to process what is going on with a mate, girlfriend, or woman of interest. While processing, a man can become detached, but may still take your calls at times. He may not text until later, or may hit the reject button on the phone until he has processed a bit what ticked him off.

Here is what you should do: If a man starts acting angry or disconnected, this is the time to be reassuring and start praising him about his qualities. You must express how much you are into him (mainly his qualities.) If you do this as he processes what angered him, then the emotional calculations he makes [more about this later] may allow him to let it go. The reassuring method can and usually works in these cases unless the action was a major rule breaking in his book.

Therefore, if he has become detached, it doesn't mean he is gone. Do not jump all over him! (I know you want clarity, but timing is everything.) Do not ask a lot of questions. Just start reassuring him and see if this solves the problem. It allows time and a means for him to re-connect emotionally again.

Once or if he re-connects, allow a little more time to pass before trying to find out what happened. Then, after an intimate moment, ask him if there was something you did that "caused him to take pause." Adopt that phrase in your vocabulary because it does not make a man feel that he must go too deep in a conversation. If he asks, "What are you talking about?" say, "I noticed that you seemed preoccupied at one point and it is my goal for us to learn each other." Next, reward and reassure him about how much you think of him in a very positive manner. "You are so handsome I never want to see those eyes look sad." I think you know how to reward and what to say.

You don't have to say things that create pressure. Express positive things you like about him: his looks, how he dresses, and his intellect, among other things. Just throw out the compliments and rewards. However, if something you did went against a rule for him, it is possible that you may not overcome this situation with this method, especially if the relationship is very new. He will detach, become distant and bounce, usually every time. Keep reading this book to discover ways to avoid breaking his rules-for-love before learning them.

Your Past

Before getting started, I have a question for you. What has been your experience in past relationships? What complaints have you been hearing from the men in these relationships? Is there a pattern to them? Consider all of the men, whether an ex-lover, a steady boyfriend, or a new guy you may have dated only briefly. For each one ask yourself, what complaints did I hear?

On the other hand, maybe you don't get complaints, but always get the same line, something that goes like this: "You are awesome, smart and cute, *but*….Let's be friends" or "I don't think we are a match" or "We're not made for each other."

Are you ever curious about the "but"? In some cases clients I've coached brush off any suggestion of rejection, saying, "I keep attracting crazy guys," or giving some other excuse. However, other clients were lost for answers and hired me for solutions.

Through these clients I've discovered how much this lack of answers preys on every relationship that follows, thus making them more guarded. Meeting a new guy, they are constantly wondering, *How are we doing? What is he thinking about me?* If a phone call or text is not returned promptly, they usually assume the worst. Do you do this, too?

Instead of silently saying to yourself, or maybe looking in the mirror wondering, *What did I do wrong?* One of the best ways to gain insights about what it is like to date you is to perform a relationship performance evaluation, also known as an "exit interview."

Maybe an exit interview with a former lover or two can help. You may receive two or three major reasons why the relationship did not work out between the two of you. You may begin to see patterns.

I will be addressing the issues relating to Why He Bounced and maybe you will see a mistake or two that you've been making, but getting answers from former mates is priceless. Make sure you give them permission to be totally honest. Please do not respond in anger or start arguing if you don't agree. Just listen, then thank them for the information, and move on. You see, it may be very simple. Perhaps your breath has a foul odor even after using mints; everyone else may know this, but you will not have a clue.

"Now let's begin talking about men by considering a question many women ask me, "Do men really know what they want?"

Chapter 2

His Stuff

"Asking questions is great and necessary, but it cannot be excessive or it feels like a job instead of a relationship. Relax and see if you can enjoy his company; watch and listen and feel."

Do Men Know What They Want?

Contrary to popular beliefs, men have feelings. Yes, there is a primal instinctual operating system working underneath that even he may not be aware of which dictates how he will respond to you. You will learn about this throughout this book.

A man is NOT looking for a copy of himself; he is in search of a woman who complements his life. In my years of experience in coaching women, most usually seek not only a carbon copy of themselves, but a man who is actually better…one who makes more money, is more intelligent, has a little more education, or a little bit more of this or that… This is why many are having difficulties finding and keeping Mr. Right.

However, still women often ask me, "Do men really know what they want?" In my opinion, and there are always exceptions, the answer is Maybe not! I should say that maybe they don't have the ability to express or explain each complaint in words. You will hear guys say that they do know what they want and know how to express it, but believe that women cannot accept the truth.

However, I've interviewed, questioned, and interacted with thousands of men for this research and have to admit that they are all over the place in their explanations about what they are really looking for in a woman. Ninety-seven percent (97%) of men in my research have never read an entire book on relationships or sought guidance in this area. However, I did find several who have read books on how to pick-up and seduce women; but on how to develop relationship skills books? It just did not happen.

So what do men want? First know that men don't have biological ticking clocks or timelines in their heads as much as women. He will want to start a family in a certain time of his life stage. The only clock ticking for him is making sure he is NOT too old to raise a son. Yes, I said it, a son. He doesn't think about having girls when marrying. A man will kill for his daughter, but most men think about having a boy to carry on his name and traditions. Don't get me wrong, it doesn't mean that he is unhappy by not having a son, but it usually his desire.

It is hard to pin-point what men want, but I do know that it is evolving. For the most part, men just know what they want when it happens based on how they instinctively feel while in the presence of a woman. What they do know is what they do not want or like.

What does this mean? Well, as I always say: You can do everything right and your relationship can still blow up in your face. This is the risk of love. But in cases like this, those who know themselves always have the strength to keep moving and get right back into the relationship hunt knowing that it was not their issue.

What about cases when it appears that everything is going great and he suddenly becomes detached and simply bounces? I know as a coach how devastating this is to women. But, as their coach, I always dig deeper and try to uncover if it was true that they did everything right. You see, many will take my above statement and say: "Phil, I did everything right!" But when I dig deeper, I can always punch holes in their assessment. It is extremely hard for anyone to really see themselves, how they are perceived, and what it's like to date them. This is why I encourage coaching to shine the light on those hidden traits that affect relationships.

Here is the truth about men.

First, they want a good-quality, loving relationship. Yes, men want to be truly loved. However, to get him to a place where he will truly love you back is another thing and based on my next point. What I'm about to share may be a little shocking, but it is also a generalization. (If you are religious, I know you have a different take, but only if you are truly living what you preach.) See "The Godly Man" Paradigm section. Well here it is; I have to be totally honest.

Tip **A man pursues a loving relationship and connection through sex and discovers the woman he cannot live without after great sex.**

You must understand this dynamic without your negative judgment. Do not blame men for being men because it is a primal instinct. It is what it is and how men are wired. This instinct is in every man even religious one, except religion can offers a discipline of restraint of that desire.

As I said before, yes, what men want is evolving. But most men see sex and commitment as two different and separate things; women must understand this perspective. I understand that you have your boundaries regarding this issue and it should be the case. However, getting a man to totally commit to you before good sex is virtually impossible. He will commit to the idea of being with you but will not be NOT fully vested.

Men also want a woman with personality because, without it, they can't have the attraction necessary for sexual stimulation. You have men who will say, "I'm looking for her inside, her mind and soul…." This is especially true in men during the ruler life-stage that we'll discuss later. However, I've never found a man in my research that made a life-time decision about a woman and their future before good sex--unless he was totally religious. Otherwise, Ladies, if the sex is good, frequent, you have personality, are appealing to his natural instinct as a man, and are doing everything else right, you are a keeper. When I say frequent, it has to match his drive. Otherwise, what is the point of good sex if he cannot get it when he desires?

An aside about religious individuals: The divorce rate is just as high with couples not having sex before marriage as with those who do. Religious people are discovering that after marriage, the sex can be a problem if he or she was sexually active before. This is mainly because sexual appetite and taste is different, as you will read in this book. However, I do support this approach.

Please take notice because here comes some real talk: I'm not talking about how good you are in bed or how good you think your stuff is, because it is not based on what you think. It has to be good to him. Nothing else matters. [There are more tips about this in the book.]

Know this, just because you think you are Queen in bed doesn't mean it equates to his feelings. You could be running him away because he is wondering how many other guys you have done this way. Good and frequent sex, great treatment, and no pressure is a keeper nowadays. It will be hard for him to bounce on a woman like that. This is what men want.

So let's say that the sex was extremely good. What's next? Well here is another point to consider. I call this the male's emotional calculation, what goes on in a man's mind: *Is she crazy? Will she start tripping? Will she get tragic thoughts if I don't text her right away or call right back? Will she keep asking do I love her or how I feel about her?"* Then he will start assessing her type: *"Will she put me in lock-down? How long will she stay mad at me if I make a mistake? How difficult is she?* And then he will ask the big question: *Why would I want to see her again?* Most men think that if he "lay the pipe" on a woman, and the sex is good, most will act out pressuring him with the "Where are we?" types of conversations, and "I need to know this and that." She will simply stress him out.

Tip Please understand this: **You cannot ask a guy to make a life-time decision on you in a short period of time.** This is not happening. It will not work. Therefore, you must know how you personally react after sex before you take that step. Your reactions will make the difference.

It is important to understand these differences between men and women.

Women Seek:

1. **Companionship:** Connection to someone to share their life with.
2. **Attention:** They want to be noticed.
3. **Affections/ Intimacy:** They want to be accepted, share feelings and be safe when their defense is down.
4. **Commitment:** They need to feel safe in the relationship and know without a doubt that they can be trusted with all their hearts.

Men Seek:

1. **Companionship:** Connection to someone to share their life with
2. **Praise:** They want to be acknowledged and to be a woman's hero. She must provide a "That-a-boy" type of campaign.
3. **Loyalty:** A man wants to know that his woman has his back and is loyal to him.
4. **Sex:** They need frequent sex to feel emotional connected. Men connect through physical contact.

The key to having a quality relationship is to understand, appreciate, and embrace these differences. However the true key to a man's heart is as follows: Plenty of Sex, Praise, Food and Fun. I've never heard of a man leaving a woman when all of those things are in play from his perspective.

What does a woman of today do to get a man to commit to their relationship? Here is a list.

- She is not obsessed about their relationship future.
- She is not jealous worrying about past women he did not pick. [Just know that he could have had someone else if he wanted, but picked you.]
- She is not pressing hard for marriage, but it falls into her lap.
- She is having fun; she is funny with a love-all-men attitude.
- She is not needy or clingy!
- She gives him space. Most men need their freedom or the illusion of it.
- She understands that there is only Full Trust or No Trust and nothing in the middle. [He needs you to bring out the best in him.]
- A man feels totally comfortable being himself around her.
- She does not make a man feel bad about his sexual urges.
- She does not play games with men.
- She is nurturing, smart, and a woman of substance who complements his life.
- She knows how to keep him hunting by changing her appearance looking sexy one-day, wearing sweats the next, hair up and down and

changing it up often, having a life and friends outside of him and not being too available.

- She is not required to have the perfect body, but is sexy, comfortable, and not complaining about her body.
- She is not sexually inhibited in the bedroom.
- She is not pressuring or interrogating the man she's kicking it with.
- She does not have right or wrong answers to their questions.
- She does not create ultimatums.
- She doesn't have "Am-I-wasting-my-time?" types of questions.
- She has the courage to speak about where she is in life--her wants and desires, but without forcing a man to feel the same way.
- She is intentional and living her life in the moment.

He, in turn, finds this woman unique and decides *"Wow, what a cool chick. I want her!"* If you are accomplished, that's a plus because now-a-days, you must be able to bring something to the table if you want a quality guy with a plan.

With these traits, you are a keeper, the one he wants to marry, and the woman he cannot live without. Again, Ladies, it is okay to state where you are, but just remember to not make him feel that you have right or wrong answers. You will usually learn a lot more about him just by being in a relaxed environment while listening and observing. If he tells you where he is, you will believe him.

Tip If you are looking for a highly successful or educated man, know that he is looking for intellect-- a woman who can handle her own business and has a plan. **Newsflash:** You will be hard pressed to find a hero straight out of movies like *Pretty Woman* or *Maids of Manhattan* existing these days. Being fine, cute, and sexy is not cutting it anymore. You have to be smart and moving towards your goals. Men are not rescuing women financially nowadays because of that nice booty. If you don't bring anything else to the table, he will not be interested. Yes, he will kick it with you, have sex, maybe drop a few dollars, but nothing lasting; and he will not see a future with you.

His Decisions

Where a man is in his life stage determines a lot of his current actions in relationships, but not everything. There is a transition between each stage. Sometimes he can become stuck or have difficulties in the movement. Additionally, in most instances, he was induced into certain beliefs or behavior by someone of influence, by his peers, or by an event relating to himself or to relationships in general. This all comes together by the story he develops of the event(s) based on how his past-self (young kid…) interpreted whatever happened and who he blames for his life problems. Often this story becomes what I call a **"global belief"** and will have a major effect on his life at each stage from then on. It also explains how he deals with women in a relationship. From the key decisions made at this pertinent emotional point in his life, in most cases, he has created a negative identity about himself that is affecting his relationships today.

How can this play out in a relationship?

If a man was beaten and abused by a woman wearing red finger- and toe-nail polish when he was young, he might develop a story or global belief that women with red nails can hurt him. We know that this is not true, but at a pertinent point in his life (his young self) a woman with red nails caused him extreme pain. How could he not create a story or global key decision regarding women wearing red nail polish when he was that young? How would that key decision trigger an emotional thought or enhance his negative story if you are wearing red nails? He could think you can hurt him. But, how could you know?

What if a man was socialized to not speak up? What if he learned that when people yell it means they are extremely displeased with you--enough to cause physical or emotional pain? What type of decisions will he make in a relationship with someone who yells? How will he behave if you yell?

The key point is to understand that a negative identity like this can limit one's options and prevent a man from having a positive relationship.

All of the above explanations lead to this huge tip:

> **Tip** **A man can bounce for reasons that some may believe are insane, but they can be real to him.** If you changed something about yourself since the last visit, and noticed odd behavior afterwards, it could be that what you changed kicked in a **global belief**; and you will not have a clue. Some men will just bounce without saying anything. It could be regarding a global belief based on a **key decision** made early in life. **If something you do or wear matches that belief, he may bounce.**

His Life Stage

Before giving you my point of view on a man's life stages, I'd like to clear up a misunderstanding being circulated. *I had a client in a session say that she was told that men go through "dog" or "player" stages. I'm not sure where she obtained this information and would never criticize another expert's explanation of men's stages. I just wouldn't characterize any of these stages as such. I would never say that men are intentionally players or dogs. Yes, there are men who behave like that, but they are the exception rather than the rule. Most men have feelings and do not get a kick out of hurting women. It is just that his nature kicks in and he discovers that this is not the woman for him. She calls him a dog or player, but he was not.*

Understanding the stages of a man's life can provide clarity as to why he may bounce. Also, being able to identify his life stage will allow you to compare where he is to where you are in your life. I love to express these stages using **archetypes.**

Keep in mind that his life stage with respect to relationships is not determined by his age. For example, some men in their twenties will feel strongly about settling down if they have a woman with a solid foundation; especially guys who are religious. They will usually think, *I can build something with this woman, and we can explore or conquer the world at the same time.* In other words, the right woman can settle a young man down and, yes, he will marry her. There will be bumps and bruises on this ride, but many make it through and mature together.

My study of men in relationships at different periods in life reveals four primary stages. Here they are described as archetypes, personifications of the qualities of each type." The four life stages are: The Explorer, the Conqueror, the Hero, and the Ruler.

The Explorer

When a man is in the Explorer stage, he has not yet figured out his place in the world and may be lost. Often he is young, but he may also be older, starting over in his life. He does not have the ability to be on solid ground with a woman right now. This man is simply on a quest to find himself. He is exploring what he likes or doesn't like; it is not time to rest his feet or build a foundation.

In a relationship, the Explorer is usually not serious; but, sometimes, the Explorer may move in or settle down with a woman who has the means to help him explore. However, for the most part, if you are interested in settling down with an established guy, he is not the one because you may have to support him financially.

However, if he is young and all of his friends are getting married, he will want to say, "Me, too." But financially your survival will be a team effort.

The Conqueror

The Conqueror has found his place in the world or has figured out what he wants to do. He has set his foot out to conquer the world. He is focusing on his target. He wants to be noticed and is telling everyone to "Look at me." If he is older, he may be in a new career or recently divorced after many years and has found a new niche. He is usually hanging out a lot or networking a lot, maybe travelling and gathering new friends.

In a relationship, the Conqueror will want to accomplish a few things before getting serious. He is not ready to settle down. This is NOT the guy to attempt a serious relationship with, because he is not ready.

The Hero

A man in the Hero stage of life has won some battle in his place in the world. He is enjoying the fruits of his labor and indulging himself on things he may have never experienced before. He may even own property, giving him a feeling of accomplishment. He may also be seeing a steady woman, but he is not yet in the settling-down mode. He also could be just moving between multiple women at this point to enjoy his feast. If he is older, he would be freshly divorced after a long marriage, looking to spread his oaks, because he is usually stable in his career.

In a relationship, a lot of these guys may start looking at a woman that they may want to end up with, but the Hero is NOT ready to settle down. Getting serious is down the road.

The Ruler

The Ruler has indulged himself, accomplished goals, and now has a sense of discovering what is important to him in life. He is the master of his world. He is thinking of his mortality and legacy. His mind is usually at rest and not wandering all over the place seeking wins or scoring. "He's been there, done that." He is settled and will think, *"It would be great to have an amazing woman to share my life with."* He wants to build a family or find someone to grow old with. He is just ready and will move fast. I like to call it the "Peace-Be-Still" stage also. "The wind and water is calm in his life."

Be forewarned: The Ruler is already established and does not need a woman to give him directions. So do not come into this relationship giving orders or making suggestions about the direction of his life. He will not be interested in you, and, for the most part, he will bounce.

In a relationship, the Ruler is simply ready and usually moves fast. A serious relationship conversation will NOT scare him away. Usually women are frightened by how fast these guys move. If you ever wanted to know how a man can meet a woman and decide to get married after a few weeks, it is because he is in the Ruler stage, and he rules.

Guy Brands

Now that you understand the four life stages of men, it is also important to understand their relationship patterns. These patterns can be found in men of any life stage and will help you understand the type of man in front of you and, maybe, why he bounced **or whether you should bounce.** Yes, you have that option, too.

It is important to match these patterns to life stages, so that you can make an informed decision about a guy. Therefore, I've included some guidance on what you should do in general. Of course, there are always exceptions. Remember to be flexible and keep an open mind. [See the following section for further guidelines: "Mr. Ripe: How to Recognize Him"]

Here are fifteen relationship patterns I have identified through my research into men in relationships, presented as what I call "**Guy Brands**."

Mr. Skilled Lover

Mr. Skilled Lover can be a relationship coach, therapist, or what women usually think is an amazing catch. He is a man who knows all of the right words and rules of love. He knows how to romance a woman. A woman is treated like a queen by Mr. Skilled Lover. But then he will bounce once it becomes boring, or after your first mistake: you broke his rules!

These guys are heart breakers, serial daters, and extremely difficult to detect or understand. And when he bounces, Mr. Skilled Lover has the ability to make you feel that it was all your fault. Furthermore, he will attempt to teach you about the purpose of coming in and out of one's life.

In my opinion, Mr. Skilled Lover is hard to please until he becomes mentally tired of the chase. He is similar to Mr. Looking-for-Perfection, but is NOT ruthless. I'm not judging their intent, but somehow, they move from woman to woman, even while teaching others about relationships.

These guys make great mates—once they settle on a woman. But so many hearts get broken along the way. You better have skills to be with this guy and bring a level of substance that complements his life.

What should you do? *Explorer, Hero, Conqueror, Ruler:* **Look Twice.** This guy at any stage will have relationship skills. Just be careful. Developing strong relationship skills will help.

Mr. Dopamine Lover

Mr. Dopamine Lover is a guy who is in love with being in love. He actually thrives off of this biological chemical reaction in the brain called dopamine: this great excitement that causes one to lose the desire to eat or sleep because of the newness of relationships. Just like the skilled lover he is a man who knows all of the right words and rules of love. He knows how to romance a woman. A woman is treated like a queen. But once the dopamine wears off he will bounce and look for his next fix.

These guys are also heart breakers, serial daters, and extremely difficult to detect or understand.

What should you do? *Explorer, Hero, Conqueror, Ruler:* **Bounce.** In my opinion, Mr. Dopamine Lover has issues and is one you should avoid at any life stage. He will bounce around from woman to woman just to have that new-love feeling.

Mr. Rescuer

Mr. Rescuer will try to save you from yourself. He is the fix-it guy and simply takes care of everything. If he is not able to help you, he sees himself as a total failure. He is a good guy but can sometimes be controlling and can become too attached. This is why some of them lose it if you do not need them anymore or if you outgrow them. Also some men in this category can become violent because their whole manhood is tied to solving problems for you.

The key to Mr. Rescuer is to see if he can focus on himself long enough to balance out the relationship. If not, you may need to move on because he can become very controlling.

What should you do? *Explorer and Conqueror*: **Look Twice.** This guy can make modifications to his behavior with the right woman who understands his intentions. *Hero and Ruler*: **Long Shot.** If he is controlling and gets angry when he is not able to fix things, beware. But if he has good intentions and can control his anger, it can be a long shot.

The Nerd/Brainiac

Nerd or Brainiac guys are very useful but sometimes get neglected because they are socially awkward. They are very tech-savvy and will fix all of your electronics and much more. Many of them live within their heads and sometimes are not able to operate as so-called normal guys socially; but most are well adjusted. They may dress funny but many of them are very attractive. A good woman who understands them could have that touch in making them shine.

They can be an awesome catch for you because many of these guys are very successful. Please do not mix up a nerd dresser with a true nerd Brainiac; nerd dressers could be dreamers who never take action in their life and are just plain ole awkward.

What should you do? *Explorer and Conqueror*: **Look Twice.** *Hero and Ruler*: **Promising.** This guy is just socially awkward and can make a great mate for you.

Mr. Shy

Although his shyness can come off as sweet, cute, and comforting, Mr. Shy's somewhat reserved nature can be crippling to anyone trying to date him. Mr. Shy will just NOT make a move. In some cases, a woman can try many things just to get him off the saddle, but to no avail.

The worst part: Mr. Shy can be all into you but will have too much fear to show it! He may even ask you out but will not show up or call. The way to handle this guy is to simply make the first move and be very direct. If this does not work, I would drop it because if he is that scared, he may never come out of his shell. When meeting a guy like this, you may have to step out of tradition and approach him to eliminate his fear of rejection.

What should you do? *Explorer*: **Long Shot.** *Conqueror*: **Look Twice.** *Hero & Ruler*: **Promising.** This guy is also socially awkward and can make a great mate for you.

However, in some cases he will never step up and can be a long shot if you are not able to deal with this matter.

Mr. Big Kid

Mr. Big Kid is simply afraid to grow up! Men of this type often do not like to take on the responsibilities of a relationship and children.

Don't get me wrong, many of these guys can be successful in their business or professional life but will never make a decision to become successful in a relationship. He may even think of himself as Mr. Big Stuff. Many of these guys can also still be living at home with their parents, even though they make enough money to move.

This guy may call you, go out, or even have sex; but marriage and family is just too much for him. He simply feels that he cannot provide you with the emotional care you need. Therefore, he will avoid a relationship altogether. All you have to do is start talking about being in a relationship and he becomes hesitant. He is actually shaking off any relationship responsibility. You should simply move on from this guy unless he becomes aware of his actions and seeks help to change.

What should you do? *Explorer and Conqueror:* **Bounce.** This guy is extremely difficult to deal with in adult situations. *Hero and Ruler:* **Look Twice.** Do not mix this guy up with a man who is a kid at heart. He can be a great mate.

Mr. Video Gamer

First, there is nothing wrong with a guy playing video games in his spare time; especially if it relaxes him. You may have the spare-time sports player and then the video-player.

However, Mr. Video Gamer takes playing these games too far. He can ignore the people in his life and even find himself addicted to these games.

If this guy invites you to play with him, then this could be something special for the two of you. If not, he may not be interested in you or does not like playing video games with women.

If he is neglecting anything, e.g. the relationship, work, school, or job then this *is* problematic.

If a man works and loves video games, then two hours per day is a reasonable amount of playing time. This is about the same amount of time as a good movie. Now, this should be the maximum amount of time he plays when you are with him. If you are not home, and he has no other responsibilities or duties to complete, then don't worry how long he plays—unless, of course, it leads him to avoid or ignore you. To be a contender for your affection, he needs to be able to balance his playing time with proper time for the relationship. Just remember, in a relationship two hours should be the maximum amount of time he plays alone per day.

Just know that research shows that games are designed to be addicting. That is how they make their money.

What should you do? *Explorer and Conqueror:* **Bounce.** This guy is extremely difficult to handle and pulls out his video games to deal with issues. *Hero*: **Long Shot**. *Ruler*: **Look Twice**. He may just love video games, but can take great care of you.

Mr. Too-Nice Guy

Mr. Too-Nice can love you completely, but over time he becomes too nice to express his true feelings. He will always look to you to take charge of the relationship. He will follow your directions. He is simply afraid to be honest and direct. He would rather send you an email or text than face you about his concerns. He is actually a coward and simply too nice for his own good. Just keep in mind that his fear is more about rejection, and he avoids this like the plague. This guy should be dumped if he constantly avoids the issues and will not face you directly.

What should you do? *Explorer:* **Long Shot**. *Conqueror:* **Look Twice**. *Hero & Ruler:* **Promising.** This guy is simply a pleaser and usually just wants to make you happy.

Mr. Ex-Complainer

Mr. Ex-Complainer spends most of his time complaining about his ex-wife or girlfriends. He is bitter and blames his ex's for his not trusting women and to explain his jealous ways or actions towards you. Therefore he may appear to be a good protector, but sometimes it is a cover to keep better track of you because of his trust issues. He must realize that the person in front of him now (you) is not the one who caused him pain. If he is not willing to work on these issues, this will be a major problem in the relationship.

     What should you do? *Explorer and Conqueror*: **Bounce.** This guy will blame his behavior on his ex-lovers. *Hero and Ruler*: **Long Shot.** Sometimes Mr. Ex-Complainer in these stages can find clarity that complaining about his ex is not good. He will give it up for the right woman. If you have relationship skills, you can help him see that he can win better by looking at this situation from a different perspective. He may just be a little bitter.

Mr. New Ager

     Mr. New Ager is part of a metaphysical, spiritual, or tantric ideology movement and appears to have it all together. He can also be a Mr. Skilled Lover. But this guy could be a sex shark, and you just might be his prey.

     Some of these guys are able to con a woman to do exactly what they want, and for the most part, they want sexual favors and sometimes her resources. Do not fall victim to this guy's intellect and way of life. The only thing he will do is deceive you into thinking that you will be above the rest by following his principles. Do not waste your time with this guy, especially if he is in a hurry to get you to practice various sexual openness movements.

     What should you do? *Explorer and Conqueror:* **Bounce.** This guy is extremely difficult and will always be broke in these stages. *Hero and Ruler:* **Long Shot.** He may be just too in love with his own movement.

Mr. Religious

Mr. Religious is a man who states that he is Godly and for those who are believers, he appears to have it all together. He understands the scriptures and is eloquent in his approach to relationships by doing it "God's way." He will state publicly that he is not having sex and will speak out against those who are fornicating, as it is often put.

Yes, there are men who are true followers in actions and beliefs. However, watch out for the "My flesh is just too weak" type of man. You see, he could really want to do the right things, and so do you, but he knows how to get sex from women and hide behind religion as to why he has bounced. "I can't be with you because you are so sexy that my flesh becomes weak." All of this will happen after sex. He will drop scriptures, or speak with you using religious terms.

Actually both of you can be doing exactly what you want (having sex) but seek to have it with those who are believers just in case the relationship develops further. Both of you in this case are weak sexually and seek others in the Church who may be weak in that category too. The thought process is this: "At least, we have the same religious beliefs." All of this is about meeting needs and not truly understanding what is motivating choices and actions.

If you are a woman and a true believer, do not fall victim to this guy's approach to the "God's way." I've found that Mr. Religious often deceives himself and will deceive you into thinking that, just like Mr. New Ager, he is above the rest by using principles that you may actually believe. He will be so good that you may just slip up and have sex with him and he will bounce. Just watch out for these Church sexual predators. They may not be malicious in their approach; however they are still persuading Church women to have sex with them and creating environments for you to become sexually weak. They are successful because your guards may be down thinking he is "Godly." Be careful, because you may be his next victim.

What should you do? *Explorer and Conqueror*: **Look Twice.** *Hero and Ruler*: **Promising.** This guy may be a little confused but once he zones in on his woman, he will ask for your hand in marriage. Just be careful at any stage.

Mr. Looking-for-Perfection

Guys looking for perfection will always find faults in you and criticize everything; they will pick on you. A man of this type can sometimes make you feel low and dirty with his negative comments, such as: "Why do you wear that stuff? You need to learn how to put on your makeup better. Why are you eating that stuff? You will put on weight. Has anyone ever said that you talk too much? Women in this town do not fit me and it is hard to find that special woman."

Every woman that Mr. Looking-for-Perfection meets has something wrong with her; he has tried everything from dating sites to friends. Run! Avoid this guy.

What should you do? *Explorer, Hero, Conqueror, Ruler*: **Bounce.** It will be too difficult to measure up to his expectations, no matter his stage. You will always be walking on eggshells with this guy.

Mr. Commitment Phobia

With this type of guy, Mr. Commitment Phobia, everything is going great until you start talking about having a future with him and off he goes. He starts to change and becomes less involved. This does not mean that you should throw in the towel on this guy. He is afraid of commitment; this is a fear, but sometimes people get over their fears and heal.

The key is to assess the situation carefully. This guy could be treating you like a queen, so do you want to give this up? Not so fast! Yes, there is a time and season for everything. You must have the ability to walk away or get over this person at the right time. At that point, you will stop expecting him to give you what he is unable, unwilling, or just doesn't want to give, and that will be a commitment. But this is not always the end of the relationship.

Too many women walk away and give up too soon. Maybe you will be the one who will help him overcome his fears, but it is not your job to make him change. Place a mental timeframe within yourself as to when you will walk away. You must explain your needs and not be too attached to the outcome. If he gets over his fears, great! If not, you can still love him from a distance.

What should you do? *Explorer and Conqueror*: **Bounce.** This guy will not be fit for a relationship. *Hero and Ruler*: **Long Shot.** Sometimes these guys will overcome their phobia and decide to settle down. It's a long shot, so be extra careful.

Mr. Down Low

Mr. Down Low is bi-sexual. The term "down-low" originated within the African-American community as a slang term to identify men who say that they are heterosexual, but who have sex with other men. Another way to describe this is on "The DL."

As a coach of all women, I know first-hand that many fear this type of man. In fact, fear of Mr. DL permeates the African-American community, especially.

I also know that many liars and haters in the community try to use this term against other men to destroy their reputation out of envy or for other reasons, and it is totally false! Can you imagine how difficult it can be to have a label placed on you, against which there is NO WAY you can defend yourself? Why? Well, it is usually rooted in a secret society of men who participate in these acts, leaving others not knowing what to believe, and there is nothing one can do.

Here is the deal. Most of these men are just conflicted and their behavior is totally noticeable. You can find them in any profession from politicians, teachers, university professors, or even athletic coaches. However, most of these men come out of prison and, since African-Americans dominate the prison population, it is obvious that the fear will be more widespread in their community.

Also you will find many of these men in the Church; some are musicians, choir directors, and even ministers. All of these men have more to lose if they come out, so they usually attempt to hide their deeds by marrying a woman to throw others off-base regarding their sexuality. This is their attempt to avoid social isolation, discrimination from peers and religious members, and being exposed.

Studies show that minority men are more likely NOT to disclose their sexual orientation compared with white men, and researchers believe that this is the reason there is an increase in HIV in the community. But if you look closely, it is not as much as you may think.

There is absolutely no evidence that DL is a real phenomenon in the black community. However, HIV is great among African-American women in several cities. It is unclear if it has to do with DL men or men who used drugs. Just like many rumors that run through the community that are absurd, the reality of the DL syndrome doesn't match up with all of the rhetoric. Yes, there are bisexual black men and some even behave in an irresponsible manner, but there has never been a widespread epidemic of such irresponsible behavior as is being described in the media. People have made lots of money off this so-called "epidemic."

The notion of DL behavior was really an attempt to explain the higher rate of HIV infection in the black community, but it has never been truly shown to be the case. The African-American community is difficult to research. It has been said that the vector that accounts for the higher rate of HIV infections is related to either the peculiar immune system of people of African descent or to the safe sex practices (or lack thereof) in the black community. However, Intravenous Drug Users (IDU), account for 73% of the HIV cases and people having sex with them. Men having sex with men accounts for about 13% and a percentage of this is from men having sex with IDUs. This makes it difficult to measure.

Here is my final analysis. Be concerned, but lose the fear! Be more mindful of men who use drugs than of men being DL. Also STOP BELIEVING LIES. Men with hemorrhoids that can cause rectal bleeding are NOT DL! You can get these via diet and certain activities. Stop believing this myth. I've seen women give up great guys because of this stupid belief. Men who love Prince, MJ, and Maxwell are not DL! This is absurd! How he wears his jewelry or pampers himself is absurd too. Just know that some men are metro sexual; they get pedicures and are extremely concerned about their appearance, but are NOT gay or bisexual. Get off that bandwagon.

Men who have been in prison for an extended period of time should concern you. Men who only love anal sex should concern you. If they do not like to give you oral sex, but want anal sex and oral sex from you, this should concern you. Men who are always talking and carrying on about gay men or homosexual terms should concern you too. I'm not saying that they are DL, but it should concern you.

Just know that it is easy to spot Mr. Down Low by simply paying attention. Do not get so excited in meeting a new man that you lose your ability to pick up underlying signals. Trust your inner compass or instinct. Watch where his eyes go and listen carefully to the things he says. Simply ask the question, "Hey, I hope this doesn't offend you, but I need to know. Have you ever had sex with another man?" Good men in the community have heard all of the rumors, and a solid one will not mind that you do a quick check to be sure. So ask the question; if he lies, you can sue him. This is what I tell women to do: Ask and then tell the story about how a friend asked this guy if he was

DL, and he said NO. Later it was discovered that he was lying and he ended up paying monetary damages to this woman. "She cleaned him out!" Now pay attention to his reaction. If he is DL, he will never call you again. ☺ You can, of course, come up with your own story too. LOL

What should you do? *Explorer, Hero, Conqueror, Ruler:* **Bounce.** This guy at any stage will struggle with his sexuality. He may be looking for a cover because of his position, so bounce! *Qualification for Ruler Stage:* However, if you are the type of woman who does not mind having a great life as a cover, then it is okay to seek a relationship with this guy in the Ruler stage. It will be just a cover and he will have the resources to create a great life. However, you will have to be extremely discreet with your relationships because of his position.

Mr. Straight-up Player

Mr. Straight-up Player is simply an expert in getting women to bed. Straight-up is a slang term that means that it is absolutely clear about something i.e. he is truly a player.

He is a pick-up artist. He knows how to play all of the cards; his goal is only to score. Once he hits it, it is all over. A good way to describe him is like a politician who tells you what you want to hear; but when you vote him in, things never change. Players come in all shapes and sizes, but all of them are very smooth talkers. Just know that most players do not want a traditional relationship and some are cheap. He may lavish you in his environment, e.g. showing off his big house, but only to score. He loses interest if you know what you want and what you are looking for in a relationship. Just avoid these guys because some of them are sociopaths.

What should you do? *Explorer, Hero, Conqueror, Ruler:* **Bounce.** This guy at any stage is out to score.
Qualifications: *Explorer, Hero, Conqueror:* Sometimes guys leave this pattern and look for a woman to settle down with. *Ruler:* This guy will rarely seek to be with one woman.

His Mental Operating System

What is a man's mental operating system? Well, how he was socialized as a kid or the types of relationships he grew up viewing. It is his programming surrounding relationships. Current research supports the idea that a person's relationship patterns actually come more from parental influences than from what the person really is or wants inside. That is, most people repeat or react to or escape from the relationship patterns of their parents. All of their reactions to a relationship are actually still coming from a parental influence, more so than from their true self.

Therefore, understanding a man's childhood will help you learn his take on relationships. If he had an abusive father, he could be abusive too, or he could have made up his mind that he will never hit a woman. If he saw his mom struggle with men, he can react to these things. You can learn a lot about a man if you know his childhood and listen very carefully to determine how his mental software is aligned for or against that childhood regarding relationships. His conversations will tell you everything you need to know if the subject is brought up about his upbringing and family. Just listen to see which direction he is taking regarding that subject.

Mr. Ripe: How to Recognize Him

Isn't anyone ripe? I hear you asking. How can you tell? How can you find a Mr. Ripe? How can you find your Mr. Ripe?

Previously I have provided you with tips on how to deal with men based on life stages and relationship patterns. This section provides further explanations and clarity to help you recognize when a man is ripe for a serious relationship or marriage.

For each relationship pattern described above, I answered the question, **What Should You Do?** In most cases a relationship is either **Promising** or not. If not, then I recommend that you either **Look Twice**, consider him a **Long Shot**, or **Bounce**. Let me explain how you can use these guidelines to find your Mr. Ripe.

If a guy is **promising,** he is ready and he knows it. He is in the process of evaluating every woman he meets, asking himself, "Is she right for me?" You have to be able to answer that question for him. But, you will have the same question. Therefore, it should not become a wrestling match, but an evaluation or testing process for both of you. If he is not right for you, it doesn't mean that he is NOT right for a relationship. Therefore don't label him inappropriately. You must have a "love-all-men" attitude in order to find the one right for you; and you should think good of him, even if you decide that he is not the man for you.

Looking twice means that you should not reject this guy based on something you did not like, or because he is not as together as you would like. He may be a diamond in the rough, and the right woman will make him shine. *You see, if a man feels that a woman can make him want to be a better man, she's keeper.* This could be you. Evaluate this guy for his potential.

Calling a man a **Long Shot** is like waving a yellow flag. It means you should to be cautious. Also, it means that he is worth considering, but you should NEVER get any hopes up high with this guy. You see, a woman can come into a man's life and shake him up emotionally and mentally. He will realize that he is not as together as he believes. She can shake him into a whole new stage. In this case, your influences can make him a good prospect for a serious relationship. He will change right in front of your eyes. The key is this: Will he be right for you? How will you see him now that he has changed? Don't make him ripe for someone else. You influenced the change, and you should be the one to accept him. Don't make him into a character, a stereotype of the man you found, that he is not able to shake. Be flexible. Reevaluate this man. It's a long shot, but IT CAN happen.

Bounce really needs no explanation. There are red and yellow flags all over the place and you don't want to deal with these things. Just bounce, exit, leave with dignity.

In looking for Mr. Ripe, understand that, in general, a man is looking for that special woman who completes him totally. Contrary to popular beliefs, men are not that afraid of commitment; they are afraid of what it has come to mean: loss of…. You fill in the blanks. Your job is to create an environment in which he feels he can win by committing to you, as I'll explain later. Therefore, he will look at you from that perspective.

When a man is ripe, his conversation will reflect it. He will be saying things like "I'm tired of this or that" when it comes to relationships. "I'm looking for something deep or meaningful." He will actually tell you upfront about his intentions.

If he says, "Let's just hook up and see where it goes" he is up in the air about a serious relationship or just not ready. But don't reject him totally. He may be tired of the relationship rat race and may have had some bad experiences with women that put him in a wait-and-see mode.

But, how can you tell? Look at his life and see if he has made preparations for adding a woman to it. A man who is serious about a relationship usually makes preparations. You will notice more responsible actions taken about being with a woman and for the role he will play as a husband. You will be able to fit into his life as a wife. You will and should notice the preparation.

You will have to consider a few factors: The state of his finances is one major key. You see, a man is concerned about how he measures up financially, or if he is able to take care of a woman (be her provider). "Can I pay the bills and provide for her?" is his main question. A man who is preparing or talking preparation is speaking about his financial situation; this is usually the main point he will bring up.

Now for your consideration, how are you financially? Are you able to hold things down? This is a new time and men are evaluating your financial capabilities like never before. If you can create an environment in which he can still be the man and can fit into your life because you can hold things down until he is on his feet as he sees himself financially; you may be in a situation to create that "prosperous man" you seek. You can help create this man with your influences.

This is my major point: whether you see this type of man in a positive manner. He can be everything that you want, but not as fit financially as you would like, but he has a plan. This man is promising, workable, and you will have to consider whether he is worth the investment. Especially if he is the type of man that will give you what you need emotionally and has the character you will want for the father of your children. This is what counts long term anyway.

If you are evaluating men based on finances, you may find one who is great and provides security, but he may not support your needs emotionally. You will still feel empty, even if you marry this guy.

As I wrap up this section, the operative word is preparation. He is prepared or preparing himself. This is when you will know he is ripe.

Also, I'm not one to say that you should totally trust your gut; it is known to deceive you at times. The key is to learn how to ask better questions and gauge responses, along with using your intuition.

So here is a short check list for you to know when he is ripe and ready for a long term relationship:

- He changed his relationship status on Facebook. (Exceptions: local and national celebrities, anyone with a title where discretion is important)

- You both have keys to each other's place.
- You've met his family and friends.
- He takes you to family, company or office events.
- You have space in his home for personal items.
- He is planning trips and actually taking them.
- You are spending lots of time together.
- He makes noticeable efforts to please and meet your needs.
- He keeps his promises and is not just doing a lot of talking.

You know he is ripe if these things are happening. In the next section, I will get direct about why he bounced.

Why He Bounced?

Well, you have just read a whole lot about men and learned about how they make decisions, their life stages and relationship patterns, how to tell when they are ripe for a meaningful relationship, and even that, maybe, they don't know what they want. Men not knowing what they want may be a little comforting to many women because they often say that they are blamed for everything. My response to that is, "Yes, I know!" Here is something interesting: Men feel the same way.

So, why he bounced? It depends on when he leaves. If after one or two dates, usually something was done that turned him off, or he could still be emotionally handicapped from his last relationship. If it was during the relationship, it was a build-up of events that assured him that you are not the one.

By now you understand that there are so many questions and a variety of answers--some that may not make sense to you as a woman. Many of the answers may anger you. I am making a generalization because some women actually get it. The key is to understand that there are many reasons why a man will bounce out of your life. This book is designed to provide some clarity.

My goal for you is to make sure you do your part and focus on things you can control, not on the things you cannot. I can't help most men; they usually do not read relationship books. However, I can help you create, learn, and develop your skills to meet your relationship challenges.

> **Tip** A man wants to be <u>acknowledged,</u> <u>respected,</u> <u>trusted,</u> <u>appreciated,</u> and to feel that he is your personal <u>superman</u>. This is what makes him feel good in your presence. Allowing him a sense of freedom is powerful too. The things you do will determine his emotional calculation of these factors. If the mental math doesn't add up, he will bounce. **"I trust you" is one of the most powerful things you can say to a guy.** He will want to live up to that brand.

There are other things you must consider:

Men are afraid of failure. If he notices issues about you early in the relationship that he cannot put his finger on, explain, or feels will hurt you, he will **bounce** instead of dealing with the issues--only because he cannot be your superman in that matter.

"How can I win?" This is the unconscious question men ask themselves all the time, along with "Am I winning or losing this battle?" Again, this is an **emotional calculation.** Additionally, sometimes men may seem to embellish or exaggerate things a bit: How much money they make. How well they are doing. How tall they are, to what degree there is a problem, among other things. Here is an important fact:

> **Tip** **Men try to see things better than they are because they are wired for victory.** Testosterone is biological fuel for winning and solving problems.

Therefore, you must have skills in dealing with men in a relationship. You must understand this dynamic and learn to establish obtainable goals which allow him to take the action needed to succeed. Being critical only makes matters worse. Show him how to win while making him believe that he is extremely close to the goal, i.e. making you happy.

Men are afraid of losing their freedom. One of the worst things that can happen in a relationship is if a man feels locked down when he is with you. Usually a woman's need for certainty creates this jail for men. It is a major reason why he will bounce. The key is to allow him a sense of freedom without constantly tripping about his whereabouts. Yes, he has to prove that he is trustable, but it will never happen unless you start out with trust.

Are you draining his life's energy? Does something always come up in the relationship, some drama when he's around? Do you have the same energy level? Or, when he is in your presence, does he feel drained, not wanting to do anything? He will bounce because you sap out all of his energy; he feels drained. I call it negative energy when the polarity is off in the relationship.

As a relationship coach and mentor, I find these topics difficult for many of my clients to grasp. They are women who are smart and simply a great catch for any man. However, as I said in the previous section, there is a constant effort to force men to connect all of the dots or make a lifetime buying decision about them within a few dates or a few short months. I'm sorry, this usually will not happen. You cannot and will not control a man. **Hint:** this is another tip as to why he bounced.

Good men have options, but if he is good looking, educated, and makes a great living, his options will increase 10+ times. If you are a minority woman seeking a minority man, and he is good looking, educated and has money or is maybe a ball player, his options increase 20+ times. Groupies will be everywhere. Therefore, men are usually wondering, "Do I want to marry her or her…?" **This is the key.** You must understand this concept and not take things too seriously or pressure men.

I actually mentioned a lot earlier why a man will bounce. But to sum it all up, here is the main reason in bold print: **You just don't make him feel good in your presence.** It is just that simple.

You may say:

- "I'm a strong minded woman. I know what I want."
- My response: I'm sure this makes you feel significant, but what does this mean? How does it make a man feel good in your presence?
- "Men are out to hurt women and are looking for their next victim. Men are this or that. Men just don't…."

- My response: Saying such things creates a disapproving spirit. If this is your belief, you will find a way to make it true. He will bounce and you will constantly attract jerks. Having a negative view of men limits your dating options and doesn't work!

I would say that over 97% of men are not out to hurt you! This is really not his goal. Yes, you can get hurt, even if you are cautious; but it is not his intent. He hopes you are the one, but when he sees otherwise, he will bounce. You want men to change, but have you looked in the mirror? Maybe it is you who should change or make an adjustment; primarily in your thinking or approach.

If you want a loving man, you have to realize that he DOES NOT think or see things as you do. Yes, it makes sense to you, but to him? Several things that you may believe, he has never considered; they have never crossed his mind. What happens when you judge his intent? He will feel like a failure in most cases because he cannot make you happy; this alone will not make him feel good in your presence. He will bounce or become detached.

Tip **Do not judge his intentions, especially if he does not see a point that is obvious to you.** Men do the best they can and deserve to receive a sense of good-will attitude from you.

Can He Be Honest?

His unspoken problematic thoughts could suck the life directly out of the relationship; actually, your unspoken thoughts too. The "I don't like two or more things about you and it's killing me" type of issue.

These unspoken thoughts are because of his concern in hurting your feelings. For example, some medications, diet pills and sinus problems could make your breath smell extremely bad, not only in the morning, but in the evening when you and your mate may be connecting. Some women's after-sex smell can be fishy, or maybe he hates your perfume. He could love everything else about you, but these things are so offensive to him that he will simply bounce. Unspoken thoughts are like a cancer in a relationship.

So here is the question on the table. Can he be honest? If he feels or believes he can not embrace honesty about those things with you, he will bounce!

Remedy: Create an environment where he can be totally honest about fixable things with the understanding that his intent is to improve the relationship. If you allow a man this freedom without being subject to guilt, you can have an amazing relationship.

He Wants Something Else

While you may present yourself as an "I know what I want," accomplished, witty, very conversational type of person with ambitious ways, he can translate those characteristics as something else. You can come across as arrogant, bossy, competitive, argumentative, and extremely difficult to deal with. Men love accomplished women. However, they are not seeking a business partner, but a mate to complement them and fit into their life.

What a man is usually looking for in a woman, especially on a date with the potential of a relationship, is what he can't get elsewhere, e.g. from his friends, family, or at work. If you don't measure up to that in his mind, he will bounce.

Now, this next topic will explain from a behavioral perspective, the why's behind men bouncing. Everything else you will read in this book will help you understand ways you are not meeting his needs based on your actions. You will learn to improve in this area.

Meeting His Needs

When a man's needs are met, he is happy. When they are not met, he feels unhappy. This is human nature; we all have needs. We each spend all of our time attempting to satisfy these needs, either consciously or unconsciously, and either in positive or negative ways. A man will bounce because his needs are not being met, or because he is attempting to meet his needs. Therefore, helping you to understand how to meet his needs is a very important part of this book.

The most effective, practical, description of human needs that I have found is the model developed by Anthony Robbins. Tony, as he is known, is a world-renowned innovator in the field of **human needs psychology**. As a relationship coach, this model allows me to apply the complex theories of human needs psychology to practical, everyday situations—like *Why He Bounced.*

The six human needs are:

1. **Certainty/Comfort:** We all need comfort, and much of this derives from the certainty that things in our lives will happen in a certain way. The car will start in the morning, you will get your paycheck on payday, and your mate will follow through on promises.
2. **Uncertainty/Variety:** The variety, spice, and adventure in our lives derive from the events

that are uncertain and unexpected. Sports, for example, may fulfill this need for a man.

3. **Significance:** Feeling worthy of praise. We all need to feel significant to our partners and to the world at large. We need to feel that our lives have meaning.

4. **Love and Connection:** We need to be cared about, loved; we need to feel a part of someone's life and to have a meaningful connection with them.

5. **Growth:** We each have a need to become better as a person, to improve our skills, to stretch and excel in our lives.

6. **Contribution:** We need to give outside ourselves, help others, make the world a better place, and contribute something of value to society.

Each person prioritizes these six needs in a unique way. For some, it is more about safety; security matters over all the other needs. For them, certainty trumps the other needs. If that need isn't being met, then no matter how well the other needs are met, the person will be unsettled and unhappy and will bounce.

The bottom line: It is impossible to punch a hole in these needs. They really explain human behavior. If you are mindful of his needs, it can make you become the woman that he can't live without. The key is to figure out how he prioritizes the six basic needs. Which are most important to him? I recommend personal coaching to get a better understanding about your own needs first and to learn this concept.

If you've established an order of needs that guarantees you'll feel continually frustrated relative to how your life is at the moment, you can simply go through the work of consciously reorganizing the needs. This can pay off *big time* in your experience of how things are going in your life. Attempting this process alone can be difficult; finding a coach or mentor to work with can be helpful.

Here is my last point on this subject: if you use the six human needs as a lens for viewing a situation that occurs in a relationship, you will be able to understand the conflicts as they happen and this can prevent a bounce. This is why coaching is extremely powerful in understanding how this system works for you.

You will wonder *Why is he upset or not calling?* Well, if you know his needs, then you'll probably understand that the issue you are facing is connected to his needs not being met.

However, here are two warnings: "Divorced Man with Children Paradigm" and "Nice-and-Out."

Divorced Man with Children Paradigm

A divorced or divorcing man with school aged children needs time to mourn; not that ending a marriage is not difficult overall, but if you are dating a man with young children, be careful. The end of a marriage is almost like having a death in the family and there is a grieving process. I am speaking from experience here so listen up.

While divorcing in 2003 and after the divorce in 2004, I was simply depressed, couldn't eat and would get in the bed and lay in a fetal position at night. Yes, there were tears. I lived in an Extended Stay until I found an apartment. It felt as if my whole world collapsed. I could no longer bathe my kids or tuck them in at night as I had before and didn't get to see my kids as much. I've found this to be the same in all of the men in my research who were divorced or divorcing with children.

If there is another man involved, it even becomes harder. There are many stages one will go through from denial, anger, sadness to full acceptance. He could also be suffering from financial issues too.

Do not get emotionally involved with a man with young kids until there is full acceptance. It's OK to be there for him; but, again, there is a process and he may simply bounce and go back to his ex-wife, leaving you behind.

Here is how I coach women in my practice. I share this: Make sure he has gone through the holidays e.g. Christmas, if he celebrates it with them, before you consider getting in deeper. For me and so many men in my research, once they have gone through the holidays without the family unit, acceptance is around the corner. For some men it could be the 4th of July or another memorable holiday. Find out what was his special family holiday or event and allow it to pass.

Here is something extremely important even through acceptance. If you have young kids, a man could become resentful to have kids in the house or around him that are not his own. Even if you have outings with both sets of kids, when his children go home, he will become sad and could become resentful if your kids are still around. So many women believe that it is ideal for both to have young kids and that it could work out better—just like the Brady Bunch. **Newsflash**: Not in most cases.

Blending families is extremely difficult and I believe that if he has small children and you have teens, it can be better or vice versa. Don't get me wrong because there are always exceptions.

The key is to make sure a divorced man has gone through all of the stages before you become emotionally vested, in order to prevent heartbreak.

The "me, too" syndrome

So many times you have to watch out for the "me too" syndrome. He will do whatever his ex-wife does, e.g. "I'm happy, too. Look at what I have" He will act as if…. but inside he is still resentful. If you understand this process, you'll see that maybe the relationship can't work. I am not telling you to run, but just do not get too emotionally involved.

Here is my last point and I don't want to scare you, but it MUST be said. **Divorced men who are in the denial/anger stage may possibly do physical harm to your children.** Yes, even if he is a good guy. Resentment can build in him and he will take it out on your kids. I've seen this too many times and there are cases where kids were abused by step fathers and the mother never knew. Just because you can't see any abuse doesn't mean it is not happening. Before you blend a family, make sure you get coaching or counseling because the risks of not getting it can be too great.

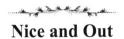

Nice and Out

He was extremely nice, but just bounced. He said that he wanted to settle down and have a family. **Please note**: "This doesn't mean that he was talking about settling down with you." Men may say these things because they are in their global life goals. It doesn't mean he is ready to settle down with you right now.

> **Tip** **When a guy makes claims about the future with you, make sure you match these words with actions.** What is the follow-up response to his words? You may just be Ms. Right Now instead of Mrs. Future. The key is to be cautious and watch out for predators. They are around and look for desperate women.

Now let's get into the meat of this book. Let's start with women's frustrations with men. Then I will address men's frustrations with women that will make him bounce.

OMG, MEN!!!

Many of the complaints I get from clients, often emails from single women, are about their frustrations with men. They shout "OMG, Men!!!" I hear your frustration, your anger, at what you see as the one-sided nature of what men really want. You tell me of the horrible experiences you've had with men and give me the impression that you do not see yourselves as the problem. And maybe you are not!

Let me affirm what I hear many of you saying to me:

- Yes, you are a good person.
- Yes, you do love and respect God or are a spiritual person.
- Yes, you are smart and independent.
- Yes, you are a great catch.
- Yes, you have lots of love to give.
- Yes, you have tried your very best.

But finding Mr. Right has been out of reach for you. "What gives, Phil?" You've asked.

Here is the truth! The information in this book may seem unfair and even very difficult to swallow. I hear it all the time: "I need to know where I stand. Why do I have to change?" Or, "Sorry buddy, I'm not doing that! You must be crazy!" and, "I am not settling!" But women who understand the concepts in this book always get their man!

Here are some additional messages I've received:

Phil,

- *Why don't you tell men to stop being cheap?*
- *Tell men to at least call if they are going to be late.*
- *Tell men to stop taking calls or texts when we are on a date.*
- *Tell men that they should stop running behind these hoochie mamas, and get a real woman.*
- *Tell men to grow up and learn some respect — including manners.*
- *Tell men that I'm not taking care of no one but myself. I'm a strong, independent woman.*
- *Tell men to stop lying when the truth will do.*
- *Tell men to stop touching me without my permission.*
- *Phil, you need to educate men to do this or that.*

Whew, and Yes, OMG!!!!

Ladies, listen up. As I said before, I can't tell men to do anything. Even after all the relationship books or blogs you've read, TV shows and radio shows you've listen too, after all of the knowledge you think you have about relationships, please understand that men are still going to be the same as they were yesterday. You can get all the pep talks you want from other women, TV and radio shows, but nothing will change this fact.

So what gives? What can you do? Well, if you want to find the love of your life, you will have to make a slight adjustment in your sensitivity and thinking to make it more accurate about men and their approach to dating. It is not my goal to make excuses for men but to help you to understand how they do things so that you can change your approach. This may not be what you want to hear, but it's true.

You must change your preconceived visual images of a relationship, be willing to try another approach, trust and follow through on some solid advice that, at times, is hard to hear. Why? Because what you are currently doing is not working for you. This is harsh, but it is the truth! If it were working for you, with all of your understandings and feelings, why do you not have a successful relationship? Why are you still single?

Oh, Oh, I can read your mind right about now and I know I am going to get all of the reasons about what men do and who's out there. I get this! Again, I know it seems unfair, and the things I need to share with you may be difficult to swallow, but they work.

You see, the women who are having the most success in their relationships understand one secret: It is not about being right or wrong, but about knowing what works and what is useless, about what may be considered effective or ineffective. Just do what works!

Stop letting things drive you crazy. Focus on what you are able to control: your reactions and mindset. You will have to forgive some of the men for their ignorance and for not being smart enough to know how to date you appropriately. You will teach him and help him out. You will not get turned off because he doesn't yet have the right skills set. You will have tolerance. You will be flexible.

> **Tip** **First Point**: A man's dating skills do not translate into what type of husband he will be for you.

Great guys make horrible dating decisions every day. When you let yourself be turned off by his dating skills, you may be missing out on the love of your life. Are you willing to accept this and give it another try?

> **Tip** **Second Point**: If you take what you are looking for into consideration, **what does the male pool look like for you?** How many men out there will fit your criteria?

Case in point: If you are a single mother in your twenties or early 30s, know that most single men who do not have kids will prefer not to marry a woman with kids already. This is a fact. This may not be what you want to hear, but it is what you need to hear. Start looking for single fathers or slightly older men to settle down with. This is what I mean about the male pool.

Most of you must change your male pool criteria to increase your chances of finding the love of your life. Make sure you look for qualities and traits that will last for 30 year or more and not for superficial traits that will change with time.

If you are a very successful, take-charge type of woman, realize that many of the professional guys you are seeking do not want to come home to a very opinionated woman. **Newsflash**: That "got-it-going-on" man you like so much loves passive women. They are looking for a softer landing at home. They seek the opposite of themselves, while these types of women seek a better version of themselves. You will have to adjust to a male who fits your personality best, or be that soft feminine soul he seeks while landing home.

Stop fooling yourselves, Ladies! A 38-year-old woman with kids already will hardly make it work with a 28-year-old man who wants a family. You will not be his first or second choice on the list. It doesn't matter how good it is right now. I said "hardly" because if you have money he may give it a try.

Tip **Last Point** I've already shared this tip, but it must be repeated: **Very good-looking men have many, many options.**

If the type of man you seek is not approaching you now, stop fooling yourself into thinking they will start. Just because you approach them, and they sleep with you, doesn't mean anything about a future. Men must show an effort in a relationship, not just show up for a booty call. He bounced because he had other options, while you were chasing a dead end.

Are you open to following solid advice? Take a look at the guys who do want you. Do you see one of quality in the bunch that you've been overlooking? Also, just continue reading this book. It will definitely help!

Tip **Men do not want competition.** Women taking the advice of experts to date multiple men at the same time are losing at this game most of the time! If a man is at the stage of seriously looking, he will bounce. There are exceptions, but these men who can deal with this usually have huge egos and their minds are extremely open. He will agree with you that men are being insecure with a little competition, but most do not feel this way. My goal is to share with you why men bounce. **Date other men while seeing him; most will bounce.** This was a 10-to-1 type of response in my survey of men.

Chapter 3

Her Stuff

*"You may see yourself as an "I know what I want,"
accomplished, witty, very conversational type of
person with ambitious ways. He may see you as
arrogant, bossy, competitive, argumentative, and
extremely difficult to deal with. He is seeking a mate
to complement him and fit into his life, NOT a
business partner."*

Are You Really Ready?

If Mr. Right walks into your life right now, what will he find? Are you ready for him? Are YOU emotionally available? That is, you do not have negative thoughts about men and you have the time and energy to put into a relationship. Can you present yourself in a fashion so that he knows that you are a keeper?

How do you know if you are NOT ready for Mr. Right?

1. Is your phone still ringing with past relationships, going-nowhere men described as friends?
2. Are you still receiving emails from past relationships, going-nowhere men described as friends?
3. Are you still receiving text messages from past relationships, going-nowhere men described as friends?
4. Are you seen on pictures one-on-one with a variety of men described as friends?

If you answer "Yes," then why do you do these things?

- Is it ego?
- Does it make you appear valuable?

- Do the calls make you feel good?
- Does it make you feel like he knows that he missed out by not measuring up?
- Does it really, really feel good to hear them beg?
- Why do you still allow contact?
- Do you believe it makes you look valuable to men by being next to other good-looking men on pictures?
- If a new love interest looked at your phone's recent call list, what would he find? Calls or texts from a bunch of men?

And then you are NOT ready for Mr. Right and he will bounce away. The research is totally sound on this matter when it comes to men. I've seen so many cases; it makes me sad.

Relationship-worthy men are walking away from you because of your past. You may be subtly dealing with men from your past and communicating with them; however, they do not mean anything to you, period! They only feed your ego. You allow them to continue to call or communicate just so you can gloat about how they won't leave you alone because of how good you were to them. It's an ego trip. This will not make you look good to a relationship-worthy man. This is why he will bounce.

To prepare for a good guy, you have to be, and appear to be, ready and available; you have to be the type of woman he feels can be trusted with his heart. If you are seen on pictures one-on-one with other guys on your Facebook, Twitter or other social network profiles, especially good looking or cut men; it could send him the wrong message about you or your type. You also have to implement project "communication silence" from men of your past; those who you describe as friends. In other words, stop the calls now. If you don't, your new man will not say anything, but will realize that you are not ready and not a keeper.

I know you become bored and like to hear him complain about not having you anymore. I know that you get lonely sometimes and take these calls to pass time away. But these guys will continue to call when Mr. Right comes along, and it is possible that you will not be able to put a stop to it in time. It could ruin your chances with that new good man and you won't know why. Do not allow this to happen to you. Stop the contact and find another way to amuse yourself and get ready for Mr. Right.

Some good men will allow you time to get rid of all those guy friends who contact you. However, there are so many who will not, and that one time you receive a call in his presence will be the last of your relationship. Also some of these guy friends will not go away quietly and can cause more trouble. Deal with it before Mr. Right comes along. Do not risk it! Get rid of that waste in your life.

Now a lot of men have told me that they like being cool with their ex-ladies. I totally understand this and have been there before. It is just that those ladies we are cool with could have problems with a new man. When she meets another guy, and I'm still calling, it will become a problem for their relationship. So again, Ladies, don't take that risk with a new or potential love interest. This is why I say that you must be successful, single, and enjoying your current life.

The "Just-in-Case" Person

After reading "Are You Really Ready?" you may believe that you are really are ready for Mr. Right. You've said "No" to all my questions, because you don't have a lot of old boyfriends calling. But you do have one, very special man. You may call him a "friend." I call him the **"Just-in-Case" Person**.

Let me be very clear: He does count. You will NEVER have a SUCCESSFUL LOVING RELATIONSHIP if you have a "just in case it doesn't work out" man around or on the side.

That hidden cushion person is the one you will pass the time away with when your love interest is unavailable. I know that this can go both ways, but we are talking about why *he* bounced. : -)

Mr. "Just-in-Case" is a go-to-guy when needed. He is usually someone who really cares about you and there is no doubt about this. You feel safe with this man. He will always have your back and be there for you in between relationships or during difficult times in your current relationship. He encourages you, makes you feel good in every way, may get you off sexually, buys you things, feeds you, but just does not fit your personal profile for the person you feel you deserve; meaning he is not the person for you. (Look back at the last point I made in "OMG, Men"—perhaps he's a greater possibility than you give him credit for.]

I cannot tell you of the countless emails I get from hurt women telling me about their love interest who has either bounced, called things off, or got caught seeing another woman. These emails are heart-breaking and I can feel the pain of these women. But guess what?

The first question I usually asked them is about that Just-in-Case Person. I want to know if one exists. To this very day over 87% of all the women I've actually had the opportunity to either coach, talk to, or correspond with, always had that person in their life. WOW!!! AND YOU ARE WONDERING WHY YOU ARE STILL SINGLE, HURT, OR CAN'T FIND THAT SPECIAL MAN? Also, this could be the reason why some women tell me, "I'm not doing this or that because I can always jump to my Just-in-Case Person." This person is always a distraction from their problems.

Just reverse this and tell me, "How would you feel if the man you are with had another woman in his life just in case?" The reason why these relationships are not working or why he bounced is because he found out, or you act as if you don't care because you have that Just-in-Case Person on the side.

What if you had a "just-in-case" job? How would you act on your current job? You know that you would do just enough and not take any stress from anybody on that job. Please understand that a Just-in-Case Person will definitely keep you from putting in the work on your current relationship. It is the same principle.

Again, in order to have a successful relationship or find the love of your life, you have to be ready and available totally and give it all you have. There cannot be anyone else influencing whether or not you will put up with the little difficulties you may experience in your current relationship. All relationships have issues; if you are running to your Just-in-Case Person when you are uncertain, instead of working on those issues with your love interest, you will never have success.

You have to focus on a relationship and allow nothing else to come between the bond you have with him. You will be surprised at what you can create for yourself by being ready and totally available. If you have a break up in your relationship, remain ready and available for a new person. Yes, there will be some lonely nights, but you will have time to self-reflect and to prepare yourself for the love of your life, and it will be well worth it.

Remember, if your love interest finds out about your Just-in-Case Person, he will bounce!

Relationship Vita

You may be asking, what in the world does **relationship vita** mean? Well, the word *vita* is Latin meaning "life." Therefore a relationship vita is a fancy way of saying your relationship history; the ones you call your EXs. You just read about being ready, but this subject of relationship history requires a special note.

Men do compare themselves to your ex-lovers. However, they will give more weight to ex-husbands and baby daddies than others. Why? Well, in his mind, it is easier for women to feel safe to cheat with them than just old boyfriends. (If you and your ex-husband do not have kids together, most men will file him in the category of regular boyfriend.) I will go on record and say that everyone reading this book knows someone or has heard about someone cheating with their ex-husband or baby daddy. Therefore, a new guy will watch these relationships closely, and if he senses a threat, he will bounce.

There is a delicate balance to managing these relationships, especially when children are involved. Your new guy will be around their kids, and they will usually have concerns. The key is to blend the adults together as soon as possible. Never have a Look-at-what-I-have or Look-how-much-better-he-is-than-you type of attitude. The best revenge is your obvious happiness.

Just keep in mind that insecurities and territorial attitudes sometimes raise their ugly head when two men meet. It will be your job to touch your new man and claim him so that there is NO question that you are with him completely but respect your children's father. Always, Always, Always, include your new man and never, never, never exclude him from an event. Otherwise, he will bounce!

Major point to consider

I discovered that most men do not like these one-on-one guy friends you may have. Yes, you see it on TV, but in reality it is a hidden reason why a guy will bounce. You can call it insecurity or whatever you like, but I've seen high quality men bounce because of a woman's guy friend.

If the guy friend is truly just a friend and not your Just-in-Case Person, and if you can't live without this friend, the key is to make sure that your friend becomes *his* friend, too. Eliminate the territorial threat.

Your Traditional Mental Boxes

It is best that you punch holes in your mental boxes regarding traditional things you feel men should do.

Point one: Some men are sensitive and require that you call them and be a little more aggressive. If you are sitting back waiting for him to hunt, he will not do it without some calls from you in between. However, I believe that he should be the dominant chaser. If he asks, "Why don't you call me sometimes?" this is your cue that he requires this to feel wanted.

Point two: Some guys are not shy, but don't like to bother individuals. A guy like this requires a woman to step up to him before he hunts. How do you know if he is interested? Well, he will look at you, but will not make a move. Again, he just doesn't want to come off as being too forward; but he is not really shy.

Point three: Men with lots of options (very good looking and got it going on) may be more relationship-minded than men who are not. They are usually sick of the rat race and do not have anything to prove because women have always shown them attention. A man like this just wants to settle down and meet the woman of his dreams instead of having to deal with a barrage of women coming after him. Stop projecting your traditional mental boxes on these guys, thinking they are heart breakers when they simply want a loving relationship.

Point four: Just because a man has not been divorced very long does not mean that a relationship with him will not work or that he is on the rebound. Depending on where he is in his life stage (I'll discuss later), he could be the type who has solid relationship skills and practices them, but his former spouse did not. He will be the type who wants to find a woman who will practice these skills and wants to get married as soon as possible. He is not interested in getting over things. He loves being in a marriage. Do NOT overlook this type or make him feel like he is rushing things; it could make him bounce. Yes, it is understood that men who can't be alone may have dependency issues, but do not judge too quickly with your box thinking. The too-good-to-be-true syndrome could be in play, as written in the section called "Your Negative Thinking." Also see "Divorced Man with Children Paradigm."

Tip Never make the assumption that a man's character is based on the guys he associates with or hangs around. His associations can range from all types including professionals, bad boys, or straight-up players. Know this, a man is the captain of his own ship and can hang with all sorts of characters for different purposes. However, he can be totally true to his woman and a great guy. **Get to know him before you judge.**

Your Uncertainty

Certainty, one of the six human needs we talked about early, is a primary motivator for many women. Thus uncertainty can drive her to extremes. Does your uncertainty lead you to do any of these?

- Checking a man's cell phone?
- Breaking into his Facebook account?
- Checking the house phone to see who has called, just looking for "something"?
- Smelling a man's clothing for abnormal fragrances?
- Breaking into their email accounts?
- Recording the phone to see if your mate is talking about you?

Diagnosis: Trust issues.

Most would say that you are extremely insecure, but some women believe that this should not be a problem unless a man has something to hide. I've heard of women checking a man's phone on the second date trying to be sure. This is simply unacceptable.

We all need to feel a sense of security that things will be okay. Certainty gives us peace of mind and assurance. We also use different behavioral strategies to meet this need. Some are constructive and others are destructive. For example, when you feel stressed, worried, unsure and uncertain, how do you meet your need for certainty?

Some women meet this need by trying to control their man (becoming a control freak), constantly making sure they know what their man is doing, or by losing their temper. Some over-eat, drink too much, and smoke just to meet their need for certainty. There are also good ways: People pray, using religion and faith; others exercise or use positive thinking. For example, saying "I will get through this," or sharing with a friend. All of these are ways to meet the need for certainty.

My question to you: What has to happen for you to feel certain that you can trust a man? Is it possible that this could ever happen in your present state of mind? You see, when you are checking a man's phone and emails, among other things, you are simply testing him to be certain that he is not doing something behind your back.

What if you were given a test that you could never pass? How would you feel? What if you needed to pass this test to get a better job, get a good man, or to vastly improve your life? But the deck is stack against you? How would this affect you? Now think about how you are giving your man a test that he could never pass because of your constant uncertainty. How do you think he feels? This is unforgivable to most men. If he finds out what you are doing, he will bounce!

Your Tragic Thoughts

If there is one constant that most men believe about some women is their ability to have strong, crazy and horrible thoughts, in other words having a racing mind. Especially if you text your man and he does not text right back, among other things. Yes, men have them, too, but in my coaching practice, women take these thoughts to a whole new level. I talked about this in another section and more in the section "Your after Sex Behavior." However, I'm labeling the process in this section as "Your Tragic Thoughts."

These thoughts take women places in their mind that appear real to them, e.g., *He's cheating. My man is thinking of leaving me. My best friend is sleeping with my boyfriend.* It goes on and on.

Based on my experiences while coaching women, I'm beginning to believe that that some think that they are psychics and can see into things going on within a parallel world, LOL. Because these thoughts appear real, some women act on or react to these thoughts. I usually suggest that they file them away in their mind under the label of "crazy thoughts." The worst part is these women tend to act on these thoughts. For example, they accuse their man of cheating on them.

At the same time, one of the biggest complaints I get from men is that they are being accused of cheating. And it all started just because of a feeling, thought, or maybe a dream his lady had. This led many of these guys to bounce.

The key is to get hard proof or evidence before you act or speak on an issue because your mind will play tricks on you. You see, how can a man prove that he is not cheating?

Many of you are so suspicious and paranoid that you drive yourself, and him, crazy. You may secretly go through your man's phone, check his email, rummage through his car at night, check his pockets, credit card statements, and even call numbers you don't know.

My precious queens, you could be hurting your man's business relationships with others if you are not careful. Stop calling these numbers you don't know, because it will not change anything.

Realize that you may have a trust issue and he may not be cheating at all. Know that, if he sees you doing this, he will either bounce or will never see you the same way again; your relationship will change. Now, if he gives you a reason to start snooping, perhaps a major change in his behavior, then I understand. However, be careful. Do not start this without cause in the guise of, "I have the right to go through his stuff because he is my man." Respect his privacy, and expect him to respect yours.

Here is my question: What will you do if something materializes? Will you bounce? Before you start snooping, have a plan of action if the results do not turn out the way you like. If you find evidence, what will you do? Don't start looking until your plan of action is clear and standards are established. You would only make both lives miserable, especially if you are stuck with each other because of financial reasons. Knowing and not having the ability to do anything about it is tragic within itself.

This leads me to our next section regarding bad thinking.

Your Negative Thinking

> **Tip** **Men don't think about what you are not, it is about what you are to them.** *My arms are too big, My butt is getting fat, My hair is not right.* This is your negative thinking; not the man's. He does not evaluate you as you do yourself.

Negative thinking begets negativity. Whatever you focus on with a man is how he grows in the relationship. If your focus is on the negative "Jerk," name calling, he will grow in negativity. If you focus on the positive, he will grow in a positive manner.

Here are some examples of negative thinking: *He is too good to be true. Something must be wrong with him. He's 45, nice house, great job, but never married. OMG, something is wrong with him! He must be crazy or down-low. He is good looking and doesn't have a woman, he must be a narcissist, a player or something else is wrong with him. He is actually looking for a wife? He said that he will only date a woman who is looking for the same? OMG, he must be a freak, controlling, looking for a slave, or afraid to be alone. He is probably crazy too!*

Why do you think this way? Why not believe that goodwill is simply coming your way and take it? This message is to tell you that your negative thinking is why he bounced and it is keeping you single.

Stop buying into the too-good-to-be-true rule. On this one, most of you are wrong. That mindset has kept many of you from getting great deals and/or missing out on the love of your life.

Here is a quick story. Recently, I received an email from a woman who is allowing me to share this story to help others.

This guy approached her and was extremely serious about settling down. They met at a Halloween party on the job a year ago. He had told himself that he was sick of the dating game and would settle down with the next good woman he met who fit his requirements. He simply wanted a wife. Ladies, when a man wants to do something, it doesn't take him long to make a decision and jump right on it!

Well, this woman had the too-good-to-be-true mindset and thought negatively about the whole situation. She said, "Phil, he must be crazy or something, He loves kids too; maybe he is a pedophile. He could be a mass murderer. He says he is looking for a wife. Why does he want to be married? Who does that? Who says that? I just don't know about him, Phil….."

Keep in mind that she was looking for a man who was willing to commit and was good with kids; and she wanted to be married too.

I told her to just trust the laws of attraction, accept the blessing, and date him seriously. I also shared with her that men are very simple. When he evolves to the point of wanting to be married, he only has a few simple personal requirements.

- He wants a woman who loves and respects him and totally has his back (support).
- He wants her to be attractive and/or appealing to him.
- He wants to have fun with her with great sex.

Anything else is gravy on top.

I know some of you are asking, What about God? Yes, this is important, and I know that sounds good to say; but think about this: A woman could love God but not have the rest of the personal requirements he seeks. See my point? I'm referring to the actual relationship with each other.

Back to the story: She brushed him off and never took him seriously and decided to take the next guy. Well, her co-worker who met this guy at the same time asked if she will be OK with her dating him. She gave her consent; thinking that the co-worker can filter out this crazy dude and inherit that problem.

Well, one year later, that co-worker and this guy's wedding date is now set. Not only did her co-worker find a man who would love her two children, but one that is extremely caring. She looked at him as being a blessing instead of a too-good-to-be-true reality. She never thought negatively about him and decided to date him to see what would happen. Well she found her king. It was just that simple.

Many of the answers or solutions to your problems are very simple and may seem too good to be true for you. But if you think they are, you will continue to miss out in life because these wonderful things are simply too good to be real or trusted by you.

You may say that it wasn't meant to be for the other woman; I say that negative thinking is destroying her destiny. To say that it wasn't meant to be is an excuse to make one feel good about not taking charge of their life. You can choose to think differently.

I strongly recommend personal coaching to clear negative or limiting beliefs. It is extremely difficult to clear them without help.

He Can't Read Your Mind

Guess what? He can't read your mind. This is something that is impossible to do and men will bounce on this impossibility. Here are the statements I hear from ladies:

- If I have to ask, then I don't want him.
- If I have to ask, then he doesn't care
- If I have to ask, then he is not for me.

Do you know what this means? You expect this man to read your mind before you can love him. He has to read your mind or you will make his life havoc. He has to read your mind, or he is not for you. Impossible!

This is a negative and actually crazy belief system that says, "I want him to already know how to love me or I will bounce." Now imagine that for a moment and let it marinate.

Most women are guilty of expecting a potential to have an owner's manual and to know exactly what it takes for them to feel love. They say, "He has to look around and see what has to be done around my house. If I have to ask, then he doesn't love me. I don't want him. I shouldn't have to ask for this or that. If I have to ask, then he doesn't care and I don't want him!"

Don't get me wrong, there are some things that are based upon home training. For example, asking for money.

However, there are always keys to knowing if someone is selfish. The key is to share what it takes for you to feel love.

Ladies, people see things differently. It has nothing to do with how they feel about you. Most of the time, if you don't ask, you will not get. If it makes you feel love when your mate does a certain thing, tell him. Why is this so hard? If you believe that if you have to ask, then you don't want it, then this belief system will keep you unhappy, single, in constant emotional pain, and—yes, he will bounce. No one can read your mind. Share what it takes to love you and if he won't do those things, then you will have a real answer about how he feels about you.

Show Interest

When he is expressing interest in you, return the interest. You want him to know that you are interested, with dignity of course. You won't have to compete with his time if he is into you; he will call and make an effort to spend time with you. Show interest. One reason he will bounce is because he may feel that you are not interested. It could be your body language too.

> **Tip** So many women say, "I'm a lady and you are not supposed to show interest before he does." Well if you don't, he will bounce. **Don't play games.**

Once you get something started, make sure that you keep expressing interest. I understand that you should allow a man to lead. But make sure you send little notes, especially thank you notes or text messages, letting him know that you are thinking about him or appreciate what he is doing. Here is the problem: Too much space will make him think that you are not that interested, but too much interest will crowd him. Hey, I never said that men are easy! The only thing that I am concerned about is what he actually thinks about the relationship. Guys could be sticking around because they are nice.

Now if he is not showing you any interest after you have expressed yours, then it is time to create space because he may not be the one. He may start chasing to get you back. You see, some men may want to keep you around just for sex until he can upgrade to that special woman. He will chase you and make you feel as if he really wants you, but he is only being territorial. All he is doing is trying to keep other men away. You see, he doesn't want to lose what he has, but he's not interested in stepping up to the next level. Ladies, it's a game, not always intentional, but you should have standards and don't play. If he wants you, then he should be willing to step it up. If not, just say NEXT!

However, here is probably your question, "How do you tell the difference?" Well, the man who wants you will be thoughtful and do the small things to keep you going. He may hold back a little by not calling at times. The man who is just holding on will be insensitive, controlling, and sometimes combative. There may be a few acts of kindness but you will have that feeling he really doesn't want you. Just listen to that inner voice and move on.

"Am I Enough?" Type of Questions

In my research, certain men were uncomfortable with two questions that are often asked in the beginning, especially when it is done online and over the phone. You may be surprised that these two questions are: **"How tall are you?"** and **"What do you do for a living?"**

Now I am sure you are thinking, "What's wrong with this? It's a legitimate question." Yes, it is, but it creates a sense of possible inadequacy. Here is why.
He will think for a moment that maybe he is not tall enough for you, or what he does for a living is not acceptable. If a man has an important job as a maintenance worker, he may feel that some women will not find his title fashionable.

You could immediately create a negative feeling on the first encounter. **YOU SHOULD CONSIDER CHANGING YOUR APPROACH.**

"How tall are you?

Here is how you ask the tall question. First, make sure you say the minimum you are willing to accept because this is a rule, and you should not settle for less if you are so strong about it. Just know that you could be missing out on the love of your life by rejecting a man based on his height.

So you can say, **"I am 5'3 and anyone over 5'5 is good for me."** He is listening and will feel good if he is over 5'5. He will say, "Well, I'm taller than 5'5." He will not have any bad feeling unless he is 5'4. Using this will not make him uncomfortable with that question. If a man's height is very important and he is too short for your preference then move on, but make sure that this type of man will want you too.

What do you do for a living?

You want a man who has a job and I get that. Also, I understand that it's an icebreaker, but consider another approach. For a lot of men it's a complete turn off and he will bounce. I've seen them come back saying, "Man, that lady is money hungry, she just asked me what I do for a living and it was the first thing out of her mouth. I have a job 'explicit'!" I have heard this more than you can imagine. However, in all honesty, I've heard this more from minority men than from others.

Guys with great titles are usually the only ones who do not have a problem with this question. They will proudly say, "I'm a doctor, or a pilot or an engineer." However, I've seen some of them indicate displeasure at this question, too.

Simply ask him, **"Hey, how was your day, were you very busy?"** or **"Phew, I had a stressful day at work, how was your day?"**

If this is the weekend you can ask, **"Do you work weekends, or are you normally off?"** Or **"I am so glad this is the weekend and I'm off work, what about you?"**

This will start a conversation and he usually will tell you what he does for a living. If it does not come up, simply wait, because he is not ready to tell you yet.

Strong and Independent?

Ne-Yo wrote a song called "Miss Independent." However, some women have been taking that statement too far. Why do you have to tell a man that you are strong and independent? Even though Ne-Yo wrote about this type of woman in his song, I've found in my research that so many men hate what that expression has come to represent.

Here is a question from a guy: "Hey Phil, I went to a speed dating function recently. It seems that all of the women I ran into kept telling me that they are 'a strong and independent woman.' Excuse me, but what the hell does that mean?"

He continued, "Take it from me, all the women I have dated in the past who have said this were nothing but trouble. Why is that statement important to say when you first meet a man?"

So Ladies, there you have it. Saying that you are a strong, independent woman should be avoided, especially early in a relationship. It can have a bad meaning, and most men do not care to hear it. You have another reason why he may bounce.

Chapter 4

The Bounce

"A man can bounce for reasons that some may believe are insane, but they can be real to him. When a man asks you not to do or wear something, pay attention. It could be triggering a global belief he has from the past. If something you do or wear matches that belief, he may bounce."

Why He Hasn't Called Yet?

Y ou just met this great guy, had a date, but he has not called back. Wow! What happened? First consider this: Just because he seemed nice, did not ask for sex, held your hand, and appeared gentleman-like does not mean he is really that way. Some of the biggest jerks start off this way. You need more data to know for sure. So don't get all excited and lose your focus. You have more work to do before you can exhale.

First, Ladies, please stop jumping to conclusions if you have not received a call in a couple of days, especially after a first date. It could be because he has cold feet temporarily and does not want to seem desperate. (Yes, men can play hard to get, too.) Some guys feel that women act differently if you make them wait and that women will become more interested in them because they did not press the issue with her. (Yes, this is a form of mind game.) Maybe he is not in a position to call or text because he is very busy or sick. He could be just trying to get over an ex; and, yes, he could have discovered that he is not attracted to you. It could be a number of factors--things you can change or things you do not have any control over. So why bother to fret over no phone call? Just chill. Do not call him! If he is interested, he will call; it is just that simple. Hey, you have a life too.

Allow a few days. If Mr. Mystery guy does not call, then it's on him. Don't beat yourself up; you could have avoided a major crash in your love life. If he is playing games in the beginning, it is a sign of more games to come.

Some guys think that women love it more, or that they look more attractive, if they tease you with their attention. When they finally do call, they don't give you any reasons for not calling sooner. Just don't buy into it because you want to train your man, in a nice way, to understand that you are not interested in playing games. Say, "So how have you been? Is everything OK with ya?" If he does not explain or say anything about what is going on with him, it is a sign that he can be evasive or too private to share. How can you learn about a guy who will not share or who is too private? If you put up with this, he will always keep you on the edge, making you think that he might walk out of your life for some petty thing.

Before you get all technical, just make sure that you are prepared and ready for Mr. Right. It could be because of your behavior on the date. Whatever the case may be, learn from it, improve, and move on.

Teasing Your Man

It is a deal-breaker to embarrass your man in public. Many men are more sensitive than you think, so let me point out an area that can create anger in your man, and he may never tell you. What is it? Well, making fun of him (teasing) in front of others, especially your family.

> **Tip** Never make fun of your man in public—about anything! Not his hair, clothes, shoes, or any mistake he makes.

Here is an example. A group of you are playing volleyball at a family function. Your man jumps up to hit the ball and misses badly. Now there could be teasing going on by other family members or friends. **Do not join in—never!** Defend your man! Say, "Y'all leave my man alone" My man is this or that. Then, stop and give him a kiss if possible.

I don't care if it is your sisters, mom or anybody, never let anyone make fun of him while he is in your presence. Now I know that family members may make fun of each other, and you can get by when he is not around—but never in front of others outside of your immediate family. Some men don't' like to be teased in front of their kids either.

So be careful. It is a subject that is hardly ever discussed, but he will start acting upset and may even be cruel because you bruised his ego, and you won't know why. He may never discuss this matter with you, but may start acting up and bounce.

How Do You Respond?

How do you respond to your man, with criticism? If you want to change your relationship with him overnight, the first thing you can do is STOP criticizing your man! Criticism only creates distant and a feeling that he is not achieving. Learn how to respond to situations. In other words, stop being combative in your conversations. I understand that this can go both ways and is more easily said than done, but taking such actions will help you connect deeply with your man in a special way. It can make him not ever want to leave you.

How can you do this? First, understand that your most effective approach to dealing with issues in your relationship is to talk about a good thing you both want. Next, discuss what is interfering with you both having what you want, instead of talking about what's wrong with your man or each other. This will keep you both out of combat mode.

Second, know this: Just because you have never heard of something before does not make it the end game. I hear this often in my blog from women who say, "That's crazy! I've never heard of this before." Does this mean that the world revolves around you and your thought process? Just because you have never heard of a particular issue before doesn't mean that it never happened or doesn't exist.

This is how you can create problems in your relationship. Just know that what is going on could be true in the current situation, and it is best that you try to understand.

Here is an example

Your man tells you that he doesn't like blue toenail polish because it makes his skin crawl. Well, this may sound bizarre to you. It is probably something that you have never heard before. Guess what? He could have a mild phobia regarding blue toenail polish. If you still put on blue toenail polish, your man, the one you are with, will feel his skin crawling, and he will not want to be with you. It is just that simple.

Next, when you criticize your man, it chips away at your relationship. How do women make this mistake? I'll tell you how: by looking for ways to make him wrong. Remember his emotional calculations.

Yes, you read, study, have great ideas, and are a great debater—I get this. But stop using those skills on your man. First, no one wants to be wrong anyway. So explain how your man can feel good with you or about you, if he is made out to be wrong and you right. Yes, you will win the argument but will eventually lose him. It doesn't mean that you cannot exchange ideas or disagree but the way you do so makes a difference.

Think about this. Before you say something to your man, ask yourself this question, "Am I criticizing, encouraging, asking a question or sharing or exchanging information?" Don't just criticize. Try to understand the point of view that your man is coming from. All of the other approaches are OK, and you can get the information you need from them. Just stop criticizing. Again I am not saying that you can't disagree.

Next, how are you responding to your man?

Imagine that your man is Lewis, a construction worker, and you have been planning a private evening with him all day long. You actually took off work to make this evening very special. He is scheduled to arrive around 7:00 p.m., but around 5:00 p.m. he calls to tell you that he isn't feeling very well, is tired, and wants to call it a night. He asks if you would be OK with this.

How would you respond, emotionally? Or will you understand his situation and have a different approach? Responding emotionally will make you focus on all the work you have done, taking off work, and will make it all about you.

Now say that you put yourself in his shoes and know that he has a very stressful and intricate job. Let's say that you respond by saying, "Honey, I am so sorry that your day has been difficult. Why don't you get some rest and call me later? I am missing and thinking of you." How do you believe he will respond? You will have just created a deeper connection with your man simply because you understood his situation.

Yes, you will hurt and be upset that you worked hard making preparations. You may be feeling very emotional about this matter. Just add intelligence to that emotion and score big with your man. It is simple. You have so much power just by using the proper strategy in your relationship.

Challenging His Manhood

When a woman is trying to make a man conform to her worldview, I often hear the man say, "She makes me feel less than a man." Challenging his manhood in this way is another reason he will become detached and bounce.

Here are some questions for you:

- Do you think that you are smarter than your man?
- Do you feel that you can perform a task better?
- Are you undermining your man's ideas and approach to issues?
- Do you listen to your man?

Here is an example: John was on the phone calling a hotel about their reservation and needed some information. Jodie was listening to his conversation and started saying, "Give them the confirmation number…Tell them that we are not paying an additional fee… Tell them that we work too hard for this.…" Say this…, say that…, all in John's ear about how he should handle the issue.

John said, "OK, honey, I got this and can handle this issue!" When he got off the phone, Jodie said, "What did they say? Well didn't you tell them this…? Didn't you tell them that…?"

What happened here? Well, Jodie just undermined her man's approach to business. She felt that her skills were more suitable to handle the task better. Also Jodie did not listen to her man. He said, "I got this!"

Women, let him do the task! Do not interfere! If there was something that he forgot to say, you can point it out in the right tone. Then he can pick up the phone to clarify or fix the problem. He does not feel that he knows everything; he will listen. Just allow him to do the job. Be a team player--not a take-over mate. You do not need to take over the task.

MEN HATE THIS!

These are ways you challenge his manhood. Men hate your commanding tone. Your man is not one of your employees or children.

Here are examples of comments and tones that challenge his manhood:

- Didn't I tell you to take out the garbage?
- Go pick up my clothes from the dry cleaner. You need to fix the doorbell; its acting up.
- Why didn't you just call the bank? It would have been the easier approach.
- Why don't you just call a mechanic and let him fix it? They know more about this than you.

One more point. If an issue occurs, such as a home or car repair problem, make sure he believes that his input is totally accepted. Never bring to the table another man's idea because it will make him feel that he is not capable of handling his manly duties. This is how women challenge ideas with another man's: "Phil told me the reason why we are having this problem is because of this or that."

He may think to himself, "Who in the hell is Phil? He's just a man like me!" Then he may rebel against that good idea only because his ego has been bruised.

I know that this may seem childish, but I am telling ladies what my studies of the average man show. It is also based on all of the calls I've received from women complaining about how stubborn their man is about an idea. Most of them bruised their man's ego and this is why they were having problems.

Now there is a way to implement another point of view, but you have to walk carefully when dealing with men. Always acknowledge his ideas, follow with a compliment, and then make suggestions.

Taking Charge

Who is taking charge of your relationship?

- Do you make most of the decisions in your relationship?
- Do you always take charge?
- Are you assertive?

At the same time, do you want your man to take charge, take action, or to show more initiative?

If you answered "Yes" to any of the questions above, then you are an Alpha Woman or considered dominant. Yet, if you want your man to take charge and have more initiative, here is the million-dollar question: "How can he?" What you call assertive, he calls bossy!

Men often complain about the feeling of being controlled, the inability to get their point across, and of being the victim of constant insults. They feel that they just cannot do things right. A man will shut down because of this.

Why? Well, after controlling everything, she still wants him to take charge and plan trips, dates, and events. But when he does, she interjects her opinions and still attempts to take over the project or complains as to how he does things. He is in a no-win situation.

Ladies, if you feel that your man does not take initiative, stop and ask yourself a question, "Are you a take-charge person?" If so, maybe he is not able to excel in that environment. You second-guess his opinions, his approach to matters, and his decisions. Please note that your way is not always better, but if you subconsciously believe this, the relationship is doomed and he will bounce.

There must be polarity in a relationship; there cannot be two dominant personalities. If you are a take-charge person and your man is OK with it, just be happy and try not to force him to take more initiative because you will be disappointed.

Giving Unsolicited Advice

You just read about taking charge. Now let me share one of the biggest mistakes a woman, or any person for that matter, can make: giving unsolicited advice. People just don't like it and especially men. It is disliked so much because of how it relates to the **Drama Cycle**. I'm going to go a little deep with you because it is needed and will make sense in the end.

The Drama Cycle is a model that was developed by a well-respected psychiatrist named Stephen Karpman. It was designed for analyzing the interactions in a relationship in order to better understand it.

The Drama Cycle has three roles that one can play. The first one is the part of a **victim**. Maybe something is done to a person or something happened. The next role is the **rescuer**. A victim may move into this role by attempting to fix something that was broken in a sense. The next role is the one of a **perpetrator**. This person may blame others for not doing things right or for not taking more responsibility for their actions. This is the most common ongoing cycle that people in a relationship can find themselves. It is another reason why a man may bounce.

In order to get out of this cycle, there has to be two additional positions or roles you should play in the relationship: The observer and the creator.

As an **observer**, you take a step back and simply notice your own behavior and really try to look at what is really going on to find a solution to the problem. The **creator** is a role that suggests that you create your own system in getting your needs met by not being part of a codependent drama cycle. You simply create the life you want.

Now you may be wondering *What does this have to do with giving unsolicited advice?* Well, I'm glad you are thinking this way.

If you are giving advice or offering your opinion in solving a problem, and the man did not ask for your advice, did not give his permission for you to give it to him, then you are placing him in the drama cycle in the role of a victim. This is because you are sending a message or suggestion that he cannot solve his problem himself; that you are the rescuer and have the solutions or resources needed for his problem. Now this may be the case; and your goal may be only to help. However, it will not be received that way because you did not gain his permission for your advice. This problem is huge in male and female dynamics. I often hear women I coach say, "Phil, he won't listen to me or my advice." They do not understand why he is reacting this way.

You may think *Why*? Well, if he rejects your advice, you have placed him in the role of a perpetrator. This places you in the role of a victim because of his rejection. On the other hand, if he accepts your advice, he may feel less than a man or beneath you, as well as feeling dependent because he needs you to solve his problems. Is this making sense to you now?

I hope this explanation gives you some perspective on how your unsolicited advice can place a man in a victim's role and he cannot feel good in your presence in that position.

I'm sure you are thinking a million dollar question: "Phil, how do I help or offer my advice?" Glad you may be thinking this. Simple ask for his permission to give advice which places him in an empowering position. Something like "I'm sure you have considered everything in this situation. "I was wondering if it is OK for me make a suggestion about this situation?" That gives them the power to say yes or no and places them in control. Another approach is to say "Hey you can reject it or not and I'm OK with it but wondering if I can offer a suggestion." I'm sure you have the picture now.

Here is the key. Don't be so pressed to give advice anyway. If he says, "I got this" or "I can handle it," just let it go because he is not giving you his permission. He is stepping up being a man and handling things himself. Do not take it personally. He's a man and men like to solve their own problems.

Fussy

Are you constantly shouting or raising your voice, complaining or being argumentative? If so, you are considered a fussy woman. You are ruled by your emotions and react by yelling at others. A man will take notice of fussy women, even if the fussing is not directed at him. He will bounce in a heart-beat, leaving you to wonder what happened.

Just know that being fussy is very annoying and can really piss off a man or worse, embarrass him if you fuss in public. This is a deal breaker and will create unhappiness, poor treatment from him if you all are stuck due to finances, or he will simply bounce.

Please note that there is more than one approach to solving problems, and your way is just another option. Also, no one wants to be wrong, and your tactic to make sure that you are right will have an adverse effect on your relationship with your man. We can all be fussy at times and a work in progress, but some women take this to a whole new level in their relationship with others.

Do Not Describe Your Ex

Tip Never describe an ex or acquaintance to a man of interest or he will bounce. He can see for himself how they look.

Recently, I watched a man lose total interest in a woman he was extremely excited about one hour earlier. Why? She made a huge mistake. She described her ex and other men who expressed interest in her to this man. I am sure she felt that it would increase her stock by attempting to make this man think that other caliber men wanted her, but it had the reverse affect.

Alice met Marvell online and they started communicating just to discover that they worked in the same office building. They both were extremely interested in each other. Alice was 5′3″ tall with average build and looks; Marvell was a 5′10″ customer service rep of the same build.

While at lunch one day, during a discussion, Alice told Marvell that her last boyfriend was a 6′3″ bodybuilder and worked for the mayor's office. She also said that another guy she went out with played baseball for a minor league team, and she described him as very good looking. This was a huge mistake!

I noticed that Marvell looked strange when approaching me after the date, so I asked him what happened. He went from being totally interested to telling me that he felt that it wouldn't work.

Alice was excited and said that he was everything she wanted from looks to personality and was still very interested. She felt that this could be a long-term relationship developing. She is in for a big surprise.

Marvel said that he lost interest because of not being remotely like the guys she dated in the past and wondered how he could compete with something that he is not. However, Alice couldn't care less about those types of men or their status because she was just making conversation.

Ladies, do not describe these other guys to a man of interest or your man, just say he was a guy you dated and talk about his character not his looks, or body, or his status. It could be the difference in you getting and keeping your potential man, or losing him in a hurry.

You can turn this around on the man and say that he needs to be more confident or less insecure. Just don't make Alice's mistake. It is up to you.

Your Projections

Are you projecting your thoughts on to a man? Are you attempting to guess what is going on with him instead of asking? Most experts think this only happens after being in a long-term relationship with a person. But, based on your experiences in previous relationships, projecting your thoughts or ideas can also occur in a new one. This will make a man bounce.

Remember, you are responsible for your own feelings and thoughts.

Projection is a defense mechanism that we all do. It is the behavior of taking something of ourselves and placing it away from us, onto others. Yes, we can sometimes project positive and sometimes negative aspects of ourselves. Sometimes our projection is the act of not wanting to acknowledge something about ourselves. So we turn it around and place it on to another (e.g., "It is not about the mistake I made, and it may be stupid; it's that you are critical of everything I do!"). Sometimes we project our experiences. For example, saying, "My mother was crazy at times but I could handle her when we disagreed, so I can use this same tactic with my co-worker when she acts crazy.")

The issue with projecting negative parts of ourselves is that we still suffer from them. In the above example, instead of feeling inadequate (our true feeling), we hurt with the feeling that everyone is critical of us. While we escape feelings of inadequacy and defenselessness, we nonetheless still suffer and feel uneasy. The more energy you put into avoiding the realization that you have weaknesses, the more difficult it eventually is to face them. Projections can ruin a relationship and your man will bounce.

Your Characterization

Once you have been dating for a while, do not characterize a man. He will not be able to pop out of character in your mind. *He is always late. He gets this wrong all the time. He is forgetful. He is constantly this or that.* Make sure you see him with fresh eyes. Remember that a man just wants to be your hero. He wants you to respect, appreciate, and acknowledge him. Saying negative things about what he is always doing, because you have characterized him that way, hurts. Refrain from doing this and look at him as if he is a new man always. Notice his improvements. Yes, this goes both ways, but we are talking about why he bounced. LOL

Just know that people change especially after awareness. Look at him with fresh eyes all the time and noticed and acknowledge his changes.

> **Tip** **Remember: Whatever you focus on with a man is how he grows in the relationship.** If the focus is negative or name calling, he will grow in negativity; if it is positive, he will grow in a positive manner.

Expectations and Disappointments

> **Tip** **Men have a tendency to tune out frequently while in a conversation with a woman.** He usually hopes he can capture the gist of what she is saying. It can come across as being rude or bad behavior but it is not. Just know that you are important to him, and he wants to please you. His tuning out is not intentional. **Biologically he is wired to fix things and has a need for you to get to the point.** Just say, "I really need you to listen now," and he will. But please try to get to the point. Don't get upset and punish him if he does become distracted at times. Have empathy.

Can you handle disappointments? They happen when you have expectations, and most of the time, they are unrealistic. Why unrealistic? Well good men have flaws but the key is that you should be willing to accept them because you want him to accept yours, too. I hope you do know that you have flaws. If not, let me remind you:

- Changing your mind fluidly.
- Because details matter to you and sometimes you over share.

- He has to listen to those catty conversations on the phone.
- Coming home and hearing details about what was done on the job, who said what, and how they don't like you.
- Hearing those long detailed conversations about a wedding and its colors and who's having a baby or divorcing and why.
- Some of you are messy, too, and can destroy a bathroom.
- You can be fussy at times with tragic thoughts and wake up accusing him of doing something because you had a dream.
- Sneaking and going through men's stuff when they are not looking or are sleeping.
- Acting like you are his mother and giving orders.

Yes, there are exceptions, but need I say more?

You cannot expect a man to be better than you, but some women make this mistake often. Most of the time women have a vision of how they want a man to act. If he comes short, she expresses her disappointments.

Remember when I said earlier that men make emotional calculations? Just know that things happen in a relationship and that he sees your flaws, too. So you must learn how to manage disappointments which can build into resentments. A man just wants to feel safe, too, and to know how long he will be in the dog house if he makes a mistake.

I'm not referring to unacceptable behavior, but issues like forgetting to do something, not listening to your conversation, or getting distracted when you talk which makes you feel he is disinterested. He may want to watch a huge play-off football game, but you planned an evening with your out-of-town family member months prior to meeting him. Some events come up without notice. How could he know that his favorite team will make it this far in the NFL playoffs? It is best that you know how to manage disappointment—or he will bounce.

Here is something you must consider: When he disappoints you, just assess if it is worth your breaking off the relationship for. If not, accept it as a mistake or flaw you can live with and don't pounce on him about it.

Relationship Habits

A man can bounce if he feels that you are too nitpicky, especially about his habits. For the most part new relationships do not have habits. However, both you and he have habits. While dating, he will notice all of your habits from how you eat, how you are at a movie, if you are neat, your patterns—e.g. if you are late all the time, if you blow your nose in public, if you talk so much that he can't get a word in, among other things.

We talked about expectations and disappointment in the last section. However, here is the key that he will consider in his emotional calculation: "Can I tolerate this habit?" If not, he will bounce. You, of course, will do the same regarding him.

Tip Men often think, **"Who made up these relationship rules?** For me to be considered a great boyfriend I am obligated to follow terms and conditions based on something she read in a magazine or blog. This is crazy."

Men feel that women often turn small habits into bad behavior or a red flag when it was just something misunderstood or extremely trivial. "Girlfriend, he dropped that fork on the floor and picked it up and started eating again." What does this have to do with how he will treat you? Making statements like this can become a habit of finding bad in everything he does. This is finger pointing, a form of contempt that quickly saps the life out of a relationship. It's a bad habit that will make him bounce.

Over-the-Top Behavior

Are you guilty of "over –the-top" behavior?

What is extremely unsexy and drives men crazy is a whining, bitching and complaining woman. It could be nasty put-downs or criticism of others. She simply complains about anything that is going on in the world-- about waiters, parking spaces, co-workers, or anything not going the way she sees things. She misbehaves in public and in private.

These women are extremely particular and require special treatment, e.g. she may need a special umbrella, a special spoon, can't do anything without makeup, whines simply because a person spills plain water. She has to have something before anything can be done; otherwise, the fun stops for everyone. Afraid to break a nail? Can't do fun things wearing pumps? A man will tag you as simply "over-the-top." Yes, he will bounce!

He Is NOT Your Girlfriend

I receive a host of complaints from men in my research regarding their woman or new love interest talking to them as if they were already their girlfriend. I know that you are comfortable with this man and feel that you can share anything with him but No! You cannot!

Even if he asks questions about your past, especially your sex life, be very careful. All he wants to know is if he is the top dog in the pleasing area. So say something that makes him think that he is your best. Do not directly answer his questions unless you can make him top dog in the bedroom; learn how to be a little evasive. You can say "I'm not comfortable talking about that; however, you are the best."

Ladies, you cannot show your man or love interest pictures of the "Eye Candy" that your girlfriend sent you via email or text. What is eye candy? They are pictures of men with these virtually nude cut bodies or muscular physiques. Some men are actually nude showing the goodies. Men in general, do not like this even if they are cut themselves.

You cannot say to your man or new love interest something about another man e.g. "He is that cute guy with the bald head, He is that guy with the pretty eyes. He is that tall, good looking guy who works for UPS. He is a cute doctor," or "He has a big one in that picture." Ladies, you cannot do this! I know what you are thinking because several ladies have said this to me already regarding their man or while debating this issue. They said, "Phil, he is just insecure!" Well, this is one reason he will not say anything, because he does not want you to think that he is jealous or insecure.

However, you may be right that he is insecure, because some are, but many are not. We are not your girlfriends and you should never do this—even if he says that's it's OK. You could risk planting a seed in his heart that will never go away. This man could walk out of your life, and you won't have a clue why.

If you make this mistake, quickly close your man's mind from thinking anything negative by complimenting him. Example: Let's say that you said by mistake, "Oh, he's cute" and your man overhears this comment. What should you do? Well, quickly close his mind by saying, "But no one is as handsome to me as my boo or man..." You get the picture. You must close your man's mind from wandering all over the place, especially if that man you commented on has it going on in the looks or style department.

Let me tell you how this could affect a man. Recently a professional counselor started a new relationship with this woman who showed him eye-candy that her girlfriend sent via email right before sex. Guess what happened? He simply smiled, but was really hurt inside; the worst part was he went limp. She asked him what was wrong and he decided to share his pain—the problem was resolved and she was apologetic. But this could have been avoided. Now, what if he was not the type to communicate his pain or problem with this issue right off?

Please understand, Ladies, men are not wired to talk about what they are feeling right off. Most are just not good at talking about personal issues, or comfortable talking about feelings, period. We are just not good at it! I understand that talking about your feelings usually comes easy for you. Also I know that you want answers to your questions fast; but, please know that we are not wired this way. Sure, you get frustrated because he is not communicating, but you cannot rewire a man's natural behavior. It is best that you simply understand and not force the issue.

If you do force the issue, you risk planting seeds in your man's heart and mind where negative vines will grow around it. If this happens, he will never see you the same way again. Maybe he will just walk away, thinking that you are not the woman for him.

It is best not to say anything about this matter to your man. Also, again, do not describe another man using terms like cute, good looking, big muscles, nice teeth, pretty eyes, good-smelling. Find other adjectives. Are you guilty of this? Just don't do it or he may bounce!

Mind Games (Creating Insecurities)

Mind games are very subtle but dangerous. They create insecurities.

I noticed something in women's behavior that fits this category and relates to relationships. I wonder if many of you reading this book do something similar. I pay close attention to these behaviors when people call me about their personal relationship. I have also noticed them while around others. It seems that many women are doing the same thing. However, when I ask individuals why, most don't have an answer except to say, "I don't keep things from my man." What I'm about to share is not really bad but I'm wondering why it is often said.

OK, I am sure that you are saying, "Enough, Phil, what are you noticing?" Again, it is not really big, but what I have discovered is that comments you make can plant seeds of suspicion in your man, and they will blossom later when problems arise.

Here it is: Why do women tell their man about compliments they receive from other men on the job, at church, the mall or other places? Let me see if you recognize any of these comments:

- You know what happened today? This UPS guy whistled at me. I guess I was looking cute. But, you know, I only have eyes for you, honey.

- Everybody said that I was looking cute today. You know how men are on the job, they look at me, but I don't pay them any attention.
- People said that I looked different today, and then this guy asked me if I was married or involved. I told him yes. He ain't getting any play here.

Sound familiar? Please know that men do this too, but we are talking about why men bounce (LOL). During my research and to this day, I have heard such comments often.

When you say things like this, you are actually telling your mate:

- You can be replaced quickly if you don't appreciate me, or act right.
- Other men want me right now. Or,
- You need to realize what you have in me.

Make sense yet? I hope so, because it may be difficult for me to put into words exactly what I see. What I do know and recognize is that men will always bring it back up during an argument or problem in the relationship. For example, let's see if this is familiar: "I don't know WHAT you do. What about that dude at work who is always in your face complimenting you? What about him?"

Here is another one: "Why are you dressing all up today? I bet it is because you want that dude who asked if you were married, or involved, to say something again."

All of the compliments you received from other men and shared with your mate are thrown right back in your face when there are problems. So again, why are you giving him these words to use later?

I have a question, "Do you tell him these things because you are subconsciously trying to get a reaction, or are you just insecure yourself?" You can piss him off with this stuff, just as it pisses you off. You are making him more insecure.

Personally, I believe that we all want our mate to know and think that they already have the best, and the reason to think this is because others want what they have. Is this so wrong? Well, I do know that it is thrown right back in our face when we have problems in our relationship.

What we are doing is playing mind games. It is just that simple.

Vague Explanations

You just read about how you can be creating insecurities in your relationship. Now I want to share more ways that men feel that you are driving them crazy.

"You keep me on the edge." This is what so many men feel or may say when their woman uses vague explanations regarding her daily life. You may not even be aware that you express yourself in this fashion. Please consider the ramifications of having your man's mind wander with your vague explanations.

As noted in the previous topic, being insecure is a major problem in one's relationship, but you could be creating more insecurity by the way you explain unknown facts to your man.

Ladies, first know that a man is always looking for outside threats to himself and his relationship, especially in regards to another man. So if you are explaining things that happened on your job or at church or anywhere—and he was not there—make sure that you provide details and names to allow him to place a person with a known event. It is human nature to want to keep situations in perspective.

Spencer and Jerica have been dating for almost two years, and he is serious about taking the relationship to the next level. However, he has concerns because he feels that Jerica keeps him on the edge all the time by how she explains, or leaves out, details of what is going on in her life; especially at work and other places. Jerica doesn't like to drop names and considers herself a private person; she doesn't understand what she is doing wrong.

So, one day she called Spencer and said the following, "I need to get some new belts for my car. Gary told me that my belts look worn and should be replaced, or my belt pulley is going bad."

Do you see any problems in how Jerica provided information on this event?

Well, you should know by now that men are territorial and Spencer's mind starts wandering and he begins to think to himself, "Who is Gary? Why is he taking the time to look at my woman's car?" Maybe he thinks something is going on with "this guy." Jerica just put Spencer on the edge and now he is assessing threats and thinking the worst.

Now here is what actually happened: Jerica drove to work and started noticing a sound that had not happened before. Spencer had recently had her car serviced and was told that he could probably go another six months before having the belts replaced.

When Jerica drove in, Gary, a co-worker who is 30 years her senior and about to retire in two months, heard the noise and asked if he could look under the hood. He noticed that the sound was coming from her belts and told her to have Spencer check it out.

If she had given him this explanation and told Spencer who this guy was, it would not have been a problem at all. Instead, it started an argument because he questioned her about this guy, and she was not in the mood for the "third degree." You see, that day, she was PMSing—whew, what a deadly combination. Well, they spent the next two weeks barely speaking and feeling strained. Spencer was simply on the edge about this event and Jerica put him there with her **vague explanations**. This could have been avoided if she had provided more details on the event up front.

OK, Ladies, I know that you think that this is too much and that he is simply insecure. You also may think that he should trust her and not act this way because he should know her better.

I get this and understand that, in a perfect relationship world, this shouldn't happen. But we know that no one is perfect. Just know that you have the power to ease his mind at all times and should do so without hesitation. It will not hurt you to provide more details in your explanations.

You can be private with someone else, but when it comes to your man, drop names, special circumstances, just to ease his wandering mind. He will love you for this, and it will prevent a tense relationship.

I know men who bounced because women were too vague. The women were left wondering what exactly went wrong. Many times, a man may not say a word. Why? Well, he doesn't want you to think that he is insecure; so he will just leave or stop calling.

Tip **Ladies, Here it is again**: It is not about how good you look, how good the sex is, how religious you are, or anything you may think that keeps your man with you. **It is about the way you make him feel, period.**

Empowerment Songs

Beyoncé is the queen of empowerment songs, catering to women and empowering them to make all types of proud statements to or about men. For example: *"You must not know 'bout me, You must not know 'bout me, I can have another you in a minute, Matter fact, he'll be here in a minute."* What about, **Single Ladies**: *"If you like it then you shoulda put a ring on it."* Or, how about *"Girls, we run this mother."* There are others:

I Don't Need a Man by The Pussycat Dolls: *"I don't need man to make it happen, I get off being free. I don't need a man to make me feel good, I get off doing my thing. I don't need a ring around my finger to make me feel complete…"*

Bitch by Meredith Brooks: *"I'm nothing in between and you know you wouldn't want it any other way."*

Knock 'Em Out by Lily Allen: *"Go away now, let me go. Are you stupid or just a little slow? Go away now, I've made myself clear. It's not going to happen, not in a million years."*

Destiny Child's **Survivor**: *"You thought I'd be weak without ya, but I'm stronger. You thought I'd be broke without ya, but I'm richer. You thought I'd be sad without ya, I laugh harder. You thought I wouldn't grow without ya, now I'm wiser….I'm a survivor."*

Women are singing these songs loud and proud! It is great that there are songs that empower women to be strong and independent and to get through problems. However, there is an attitude that comes with these songs that men will simply not want to deal with and they will bounce.

Men are looking for a soft safe landing, not a fight. Some of these songs prepare women for a fight. Sing and enjoy the songs, but check the attitude in the presence of a man.

May I suggest another theme song for you, an antidote to these songs which tear you and your man apart? Why must your strength make him weak? Tammy Wynette's **"Stand by Your Man"** tells of another way to be a strong woman, standing firm against the jealous and self-serving people who would have you criticize your man, just when he needs you the most. *Stand by your man. Give him two arms to cling to and something warm to come to when nights are cold and lonely. Stand by your man, and show the world you love him. Keep giving all the love you can. Stand by your man*

Moochers

"I want someone in my life. Men just see me as a friend. Men just leave without saying anything. I'm a good person and help others out, so why I can't I find someone special who will stick around?"

Have you asked yourself these questions? If not, then this message is NOT for you.

But I discovered an interesting pattern with good caring women who just can't seem to keep a man interested. They have no problems meeting new men. It is just that, when they do, they are usually quickly placed in the friends' category, or he just bounces.

Are you ready for this? Well, it is because of "moochers." Those people who you lend money to, allow to stay with you on and off, or maybe that doing-nothing brother or son--all able-bodied grown-ups who are just taking.

When a man assesses a woman for consideration, he looks at her relationships for possible conflicts. He will appreciate the fact that you are a caring and good person, but will NOT like your always putting yourself out and doing things for your able-bodied, mooching family members. He usually will NEVER say anything about this to you, but will say to himself, "This is not the woman for me" and move on.

You may ask, "What do you mean 'doing things for'?" Well,

- Paying bills for them
- Allowing them to use your checking account to deposit money and have you writing checks for them
- Preparing meals for them
- Giving them keys to your place and allowing them to come over, go into YOUR fridge, and hang out
- Helping them find a new place and cleaning it up
- Going with them for business transactions
- Just doing things that grown folks, especially men, should do for themselves.

If you have people in your life like this, and especially if they are men, most quality men will keep on stepping and will put you in the friends' category! You will not be the woman he will want to spend his life with. A man cannot have this going on in his household, even if it is your own money! He will not have the heart to come between you and that family member. Therefore he will bounce.

Prepare your life for a quality man and clean this stuff up. Stop doing these things for able-bodied grown folk. Don't get me wrong, it is okay to help, but not to be totally engaged in doing things for these functioning, grown moochers.

Freeloading Friends

I have always been curious as to why so many women have to show proof to their friends that their man is good. I mean there is a salesperson type of approach to selling their mate to others. I guess wanting others to like your mate or to be happy for you is normal human behavior.

They will tell their friends, e.g., "He took me here, or there. He did this for me; he did that for me. My man is this or that. He bought me this and that."

This kind of talk always leads to one worse thing: freeloading friends. This is when your girlfriends ask you and your man out so that they can get FREE drinks or dinner. Also these girlfriends or family members will ask you and your man to take them on a trip so that he can pick up the tab. Freeloading girlfriends!

Here is a story for you

Kyle and Emma have been dating for several months now; it is going quite well. However, Emma's friends are really suspicious of Kyle simply because he seems too good to be true. He is very attentive, thoughtful, and quite caring.

Emma's best friends, Kim and Diana, simply do not like Kyle and it is driving her crazy. These are her girls, road dogs, and the ones she's been hanging with all of her life. She wants her friends to be happy for her but they are not there yet.

Kyle decided to purchase tickets for all of them to see Beyoncé and Robin Thicke in concert at St. Pete Times Forum in Tampa, Florida. When they found out, they were so elated and jumped for joy!

So off to the concert they went. It was a hot July night and unforgettable. They sang all night long, including Beyoncé's "You must not know 'bout me, you must not know 'bout me, I can have another you by tomorrow, So don't you ever for a second get to thinkin' You're irreplaceable…." Robin Thicke was the bomb too.

The next day, Kim calls Emma and says, "You know, Kyle is not bad after all. I think he really cares about you and I like him now." Emma jumped up and shouted with excitement! WHEW!

Guess what happened next? Kim and Diana would call Emma all the time about going to new restaurants and out of town events. "Hey, girl, why don't you and Kyle join us here…or there…" Do you know why? They expected Kyle to pick up the tab for every evening!

Emma felt so much pressure that she would slip him money so that it could appear that he was funding the night. Kyle did not like this; it created distance in the relationship. Emma was happy because she felt that everything was coming together and that the relationship was getting stronger.

Well, suddenly Kyle pulled away from her and did not explain why. He told her that the relationship was moving in a direction that he was not expecting. He also said that she was wonderful, but it was not working for him. Emma was devastated!

She felt that things were going great and could not figure out what was the problem. But as you read this story, you know the problem: those free-loading friends that were destroying the relationship.

How could Kyle ask Emma to choose between her childhood friends and him? It wasn't going to happen. He never even mentioned it; just pulled away. Kim and Diana comforted her and said, "I knew that he was just like the others. He is a dog and afraid of commitment." To this very day, this cycle of nonsense is still going on in that circle.

Kyle is now engaged to be married to a wonderful woman who does not allow her friends to come between their love.

So Ladies, you just learned another reason some men may stop calling or simply bounce. Do not let your freeloading friends or family members run a good man away.

Meddling

We have been discussing some of the ways in which you can contribute to a man's bouncing right out of your life and how to prevent it. From how you can challenge his manhood by trying to make him conform to your world view to responding to him critically and indulging your trust issues, but it can go a little further.

Now, let's consider complications added to your relationship challenges by others in your life: Family, friends, old boyfriends or ex's.

If you really want a man to bounce, allow others to meddle, to butt into your relationship. Ladies, some of you have family members messing in your relationship. You know who they are, it could be your sister, brother, cousin, uncle or aunt. Or, perhaps friends in whom you usually confide.

Are any of them calling, wanting details about what is going on in your relationship? And do you call any of them, telling them your business, especially when there are problems? This encourages their meddling. Stop it.

Be aware of anyone in your life who is always butting in, calling and lying, saying that someone said this or that and it is not true. They are just simply plain ole messy. You need to put them in their place, or risk losing your man.

As I said, in "Challenging His Manhood," one of the worst things you can do to your man is to second-guess his opinions or advice by seeking new ones from another man. This really bruises a man's ego; and yet women do it all the time. I don't care if it is your father; never do that in his presence. If you feel that your man's opinion or advice is not on solid ground, just don't let on that you sought opinions elsewhere. Protect his sense of manhood all the time.

A big complaint I've received from men is that their woman never takes their advice. They tell me, "I told her the same thing but she won't' listen to me." Ladies, try to avoid this behavior because it hurts your man.

Here is a quick, true story

Marshall and Troy had been together for one year but one day Troy suddenly bounced out of the relationship very angry. According to Marshall, she did not have a clue what was the problem in the relationship, even though Troy had given her a heads up on his concern. However, Troy was quiet and not very talkative. He didn't say things over and over again, but loved Marshall. Here is the story.

Marshall's car broke down and Troy took action to get the vehicle fixed and arranged transportation. When her father found out, he called Troy and wanted details on what action he was taking to resolve the problem. He replied, "Mr. Hatten, I have everything taken care of. I took her vehicle to MetroPlex Automotive." Marshall's dad said, "I've never heard of this company and do not want my daughter stranded because you are using a shade-tree mechanic."

Troy explained that his family has used this company for many years and that they have an impeccable reputation for quality and price. He said, "They are considered a gem in the automotive repair industry."

Marshall's dad said, "Well, what's their location and phone number, I want to call the Better Business Bureau to see if they have any complaints." Then he asked Troy, "What problem did they find with the vehicle?" These types of comments had been going back and forth constantly throughout their relationship.

Troy told Marshall on several occasions that he did not like this, but she felt that her dad was just concerned and loved her. He said, "Yeah, I know, but I've got this. I provide here. I pay the bills, not your dad." She responded by saying, "Oh Troy, you should get over it and stop being so insecure."

Well, Troy bounced because he had taken all he could. Marshall was extremely hurt, but to this very day she believes that he was insecure and wrong.

Ladies, can you see what is wrong with this picture? Instead of letting her dad butt in, she should have told him how much he is loved and appreciated. She should have explained to her dad that Troy is the man looking after her now.

Why He Stopped Calling

We have discussed a man's not calling a lot. I will now add to this subject, speaking directly about why he stopped calling.

If a man feels that it is hard to make you happy, or that it is a lot of work, he will stop calling. I'm going to continue to repeat this: "**Men like being around people who make them feel good.**" A man will watch a game with you if you make him feel good about it. You need to be fun to hang out with.

A friend was introduced to this nice lady who was smart, educated, funny, outgoing, and made him feel pretty good at first. Their conversations were great. He would call her often during the day and she called him — hey, he was interested.

This was the initial stage of the relationship and suddenly he stopped calling. When she called him, he just clicked "ignore." He was conflicted, but still somewhat interested. She texted him and he did not respond. He was trying to collect his thoughts. Then he texted her and said that he would call her tomorrow. He simply needed a break. Before you get mad keep reading.

The next day, he called her and she was noticeably irritable and began to ask him a series of questions. He cut her off because of a meeting and said that he would call her back. He believed in keeping his word, so he called her back and she started again. He said right then, "I am sorry but this is not working for me. I think that you are a nice person, but not the one for me."

I am sure that she was baffled and bewildered, but it was how he felt and he wasn't going to lead her on. She said, "I am through with men, I felt that you would be different." She hung up the phone. He was going to explain his reasons in detail but she did not allow him to; well she never listened attentively anyway, unless he was answering her questions.

Why did he stop calling?

1. She started nagging all the time and was moving very fast and demanding: When are we...? How long will it be...? I would love to have this... I can't wait until we take our first weekend trip...A man has to get me at least three carats if he wants to marry me...
2. He was thinking that he could not afford her.
3. She was too much work: When he was with her, she had the overly talking bug and it was the nagging again with all the questions without any room to breathe. She was not a good listener.
4. She did not have time for a relationship and worked too much.
5. Her lifestyle was not conducive to having a relationship.
6. She did not know how to simply hang out in a relaxed setting without getting to the business of the relationship. "I need to know this and tell me about that..." It was a job interview, not a relationship.

I know that you have read books that say that you must gather information from men, but Ladies, there is a way to do this without interrogating or making yourself less attractive.

He wasn't forcing her to do anything or to jump into bed. He wanted someone who can be relaxed, have fun, have great conversations, and learn about him in this setting. It was like she was an attorney during a cross-examination.

Two weeks passed and he decided to call her to explain his reasons for not calling. This could have been a great exit interview. He felt that maybe she would be calm by then. Well the girlfriend peer pressure talking points kicked in, you know this "strong-independent-woman stuff," and she was angry and non-responsive.

He clearly stated that this was not an attempt to get back into her life; it was just for her to know that they could not get those moments back again. There was a seed planted in his head early that will not go away. Therefore he felt that they could help each other by explaining their actions, if she was interested. He told her what was just explained here.

Her comments: "I am sorry! I am going to be me. I have been hurt too many times not to understand a guy and get all of the information that I need, when I need it."

Again, she was smart, educated, funny at times and outgoing, but simply was too much work. He did not feel good in her presence because it was work and no fun. He did not want to hang-out with her again; he felt that she would never listen to his concerns or desires. He felt her goal was information, and she wasn't willing to balance her need for information with what he wanted: answering relationship questions in a relaxed setting. This is why he stopped calling. It has now been three years and she is still going through this cycle.

Relationship books have given her more ammunition, because many of them include the main questions every woman should ask before getting too deep into a relationship. These books are her Bible now. She feels vindicated. I simply believe that some individuals will use whatever they can to support that failed argument. I haven't read any relationship book that says you should be an aggressive interrogator without having fun.

Getting back to this story, do you want to know what he did to prevent this? When she would get off into this questioning mode her reason was, "because I just need to know." He would change the subject to a TV show or some other current event, anything other than their conversation. He would say, "Can we talk about something else because I've been having serious talks all day and want to relax now." What was her response? Okay. Then ten (10) minutes later she would go back to the questioning again. It was no fun for him. She did not make him feel good; he did not want to hang out with her.

> **Tip** **Asking questions is great and necessary, but it cannot be excessive or it feels like a job instead of a relationship.**

Men like someone who they can hang-out with, too, and if you are interrogating all the time, then it's a no go.

Talking and interrogation are two different things. What she wanted was her questions answered all at once in order to make a decision about him. What decision? There was nothing on the table yet but intrigue and this started less than a week before. Now she wanted to force a relationship by demand, without knowing if they could actually enjoy each other's company in person. She actually wanted the same thing he did—a loving relationship—but she did not know how to get there.

Women need to understand this: Just because you want to know doesn't mean that you will get an answer that day. If you force it, the door could get shut permanently.

"Men instinctively conceal their intentions because they are hunters and warriors. They are not attempting to be secretive or to lie; they just don't want to show their hand. If a warrior shows an aggressor his hand, he will not survive. You must understand this dynamic and stop believing that men just lie."

Chapter 5

Getting Intimate

*"Lack of sexual spontaneity is frustrating to men.
You have to be able to sneak a quickie to take the
edge off your man from time to time, or he will bounce."*

Are You Deluding Yourself?

- Men tell me that my stuff is sooo good.
- Men tell me all the time that I look good.
- Men tell me all the time that I am...
- Men tell me this all the time.
- Men tell me that all the time.

Is it real?

I know we all need to have self-confidence and self-worth, but what I have been hearing from men is interesting. They say that women are using those words above as a weapon. The goal of women, as men have shared, is to make men feel inadequate; especially, if they simply disagree with another man's findings.

Ladies, just because you have received a few compliments (sincere or flattery), or at least not heard any negative comments about something that you do or wear, does not mean it is acceptable to all men. Also, it does not mean that you do that thing well, or look good in what you are wearing. You may be suffering from a false belief, a delusion.

Tip **What is NOT good to one man can be absolutely wonderful to another.** Just stop thinking that it is good to ALL.

What I am referring to is the arrogance that feeds delusions. YES, I know that this goes both ways, but again we are talking here about what men want.

Stop making a man feel that he is wrong for having an opinion that is different from another man; many of you have this bad!

Here is a story for you. Eddie complained that Brooke simply would not listen and always did a certain thing that drives him crazy. Now, I am not going to tell you what it was that she was doing in order to keep their identities secure. Guess what Brooke said to me? "Well, Phil, men in the past have told me that they love this and that…"

I asked Brooke who she is with now. She said, "Eddie." I then said, "Well, Eddie doesn't like this. Is this something you can live without?" She said, "Well, I don't know why he does not like this when other men do." Delusions!

Brooke was arrogant enough to think that Eddie was wrong. She believes that Eddie doesn't want a strong woman.

Men are telling me that women are becoming more and more delusional, that they "got it going on." You know what? Men's thought processes are not even there about this stuff. They just want a good woman who shares their dreams and goals in life among other things. Women, you want the same thing, too. So, where did this strong independent woman stuff originate?

I ask that each of us look at our life and realize that we have faults and do not have all the answers. What I may like, someone else will not. It doesn't make me wrong, but if I want to be with that person, I will either have to adjust, or move on. You cannot force someone to like something just because you think that you are good at it. You may not be that good; it could be a delusion, someone flattering you in order to get what they wanted. Another reason why he bounced!

Sexual Appetite

- Not enough sex.
- A woman who is ashamed of her body.
- A woman complaining about body parts.
- A woman that is not liberated in the bedroom.
- Women who cannot receive.

These are the main complaints of men. Based on my experience, one of the main reasons why a man will bounce has to do with one's sexual appetite or a lack of sexual desire. However, this is the most under-discussed topic with couples.

For example, there are so many women who just want to give and give in the bedroom but cannot receive. A man has a strong need to accomplish a major goal while in the bedroom.

> **Tip** **A man needs and wants you to reach an orgasm**, bust a nut, or to cum (whatever phrase you like to use). He understands that there will be times that you will not, but this has to be the exception.

His ego is tied to his performance in the bedroom and men keep score. Winning means you cum! Losing means you did not cum. Therefore, you must learn how to receive, so that he can give or perform. The end is that he can give you what he believes is a massive orgasm.

Whether we like to acknowledge it or not, our sexual appetite underlies much of what we do. It underlies why men are concerned about status and height, and why women are more concerned about being beautiful and about their appearance. It is human nature, how we evolved as a species. Our behavior was shaped by our past and in order for us to survive, we have to reproduce. Believe it or not, Nature does not care how we populate the earth and reproduce, just as long as it is done; and this process shapes our sexual behavior.

Nowadays individuals, especially men, are forced to live by rules that go against their natural tendencies.

The number one complaint of men is that they are not getting enough sex, that they are forced to use will power and self-restraint to tame their desires. Here is the problem: It is not natural. This is why so many get caught in cheating, among other things. If you are not willing to address your mate's sexual appetite and his willingness to suppress it, your relationship MAY lead to infidelity, or he will bounce, and that is a fact.

Please Note: Compromising only works to a point as long as it suppresses the mate's desire enough that will power and self-restraint is more manageable. However, if the compromise is not suppressing that sexual appetite enough, they will go elsewhere.

In my coaching practice, I address the sexual appetite issue directly and up close. I do not allow one mate to create excuses as to why they are more sexually reserved. I explain to them that whether or not their mate understands the situation does not deter the appetite; the desire is still there. I ask them, **What do you expect them to do?**

Allow your mate to be open and upfront about his sexual appetite. Do not be ashamed of your body and complain about body parts. This is unattractive to men.

Tip **Lack of sexual spontaneity is frustrating to men.** You have to be able to sneak a quickie to take the edge off your man from time to time, or he will bounce.

"I like it, but it is too much trouble trying to get it." This is a complaint men have about women who can not be spontanous. Everything has to be in order if you are going to have sex. It takes so long that he will not want to go through the trouble. Guys have complained about wanting their woman for a quickie to take the edge off, but she would not because the time was not right for her. Men love women who can sneak in the bathroom or closet for a quickie-- even if people are around. Just being able to sneak is a major turn-on for men; without this sexual spontaneity, most guys will bounce. You will NOT be the woman he can't live without.

The Waiting Rule

Do you believe that women are rewarded for making a man wait for sex? It is rare that a woman is rewarded for making him wait too long. This is simply a fact revealed by my research (not including those waiting for religious purposes). But please understand this: Men will look for sex first and then stumble on love; while women usually search for love first.

Many advise women to have a 30-, 60-, or 90-day waiting rule. I was guilty of recommending this, too, until I performed actual research and my findings did not support this waiting rule. So most of these advisers are telling you what they think is best because no one really knows.

Now a lot of advisers or coaches believe that they know how men think and many actually are on point. I love all the ideas that are out there regarding waiting, but I believe on this subject many are telling you only what they think is best for you and it really makes sense because I used to believe the same.

However, I've interviewed hundreds, surveyed and interacted with thousands of men on social media, asking these questions:

1. How long did your woman make you wait?
2. If you waited long, what was the outcome?
3. If you did not wait long, did you think that she was less of a lady by not making you wait?

4. Why do you feel that women want you to wait?

Now there is also a biblical and moral perspective on this, but I exempted those responses from this research.

What was the end result? Nothing, really—but interesting!

As I said before, men are wired differently because they search for sex and stumble on love. You see, men are totally aware that you want to be ladylike. They are totally aware that women have self-respect. They also know that women are concerned about what men think of them in this matter.

What do men actually think? Nothing! Why? Because if he digs you, and the time is right, it is right from his perspective! Men do not judge your character in this matter. Now if you do some really freaky stuff, he will have an opinion. Men can always tell a true lady from those who are simply loose or as they put it "a true ho," as so many of them said in my research.

What happened when a woman made a man wait for a long time? There was a tremendous buildup—followed, usually, by a letdown. I've heard more cases of this than ever! Huge letdown!

Now from a practical perspective, if the moment is right, and you are feeling each other, it is OK to allow nature to take its course—if it is within your values. But only if you feel you know him and have a good understanding of his character. However, I believe that a woman should give **at least a full two weeks** before jumping into a bed with a man. This allows you the opportunity to have several dates and understand his intentions.

You see, Ladies, men cannot take too much frustration in that matter if he feels that it's the right time for him. But he can be patient.

Now if he builds the love up and is not able to put that passion toward you, it will become a letdown (blue balls). It will be hard for him to build it up again in that way for fear that nothing will happen. He also may direct that passion toward someone else.

Guess what happens? Something changes; he feels it's a game he must win. I just know that the actual act he's been waiting for becomes a letdown. Also in most cases, women become hurt. He will ask himself, "I was waiting for this?" The total act was not what he expected and sometimes it's the same for women, especially if she brags about giving him a night to remember.

What happened? I don't know, but all I can say is that the man had too many build-ups with nothing happening. Then he stops calling because he is not able to tell you that it was not right for him.

This was the common denominator for men in my research. It was also the main reason men said that they did not call a woman back—the sex was a big letdown. "She made me think that her stuff was well worth waiting for when it was not." I guess it was too much expectation. Call it silly, but this is what the research reveals. Or it was another case of a woman deluding herself, having been led on by a greedy lover.

OK, Ladies, so you wanted to know what men think about waiting? Well it is here and it is up to you to figure out how to apply the knowledge. I just want you to be equipped with information.

The key is to never allow him to build up sexually and then not let anything happen. Now keep in mind that every man is different. Some men need to totally connect mentally before anything sexual can happen, so do not rush these types. What I do know is that you can lose if you wait too long and in many cases 90 days is a relationship killer. I don't care what anyone else tells you about this.

Tip **Make sure you truly know that he is interested in you before sex.** Also, get to know him before you even go there. If you make him wait, just do not allow passionate build up to take place if nothing is going to happen. The way to keep it interesting, if he gets excited, is to say, "I know you are turned on and I want to give you a night to remember, but I only have sex with my boyfriend." This is not pressuring a man for a life-time commitment while letting him know that you have standards.

Unguarded Behavior

Here is a perspective that most NEVER understand and another reason why men bounce. How are you when you are **guarded**? How are you when you have **unguarded**? Is there a difference? When getting to know a man, most women will often say "My guards are up." But they never truly understand what this means. As I said before, it means that a woman is seeking certainty before anything else. She needs to be certain that he is not....[whatever she is not looking for.] She is putting her need for certainty first.

Now I understand this behavior and the reason behind it, but your demeanor must be fun while being a little cautious with a stranger. In many cases women never understand how timing and change in emotions can play in this scenario.

Here is an example for you.

First, her guards are up with the goal of remaining safe, while he is playing this wait-and-see game with her. They are feeling each other out, and maybe he is seriously seeking a lasting relationship. She is making this guy pay for her past hurts and previous relationships. The only reason to be guarded is to avoid repeating a problem that happened in the past with other guys. You are actually turning the man in front of you into a negative suspect based on your life experiences with guys in the past.

He remains patient because he likes you. Who is this person that he sees? It's a guarded you, maybe extremely fun and interesting with an excellent personality. BUT, he doesn't really know how you are when you are unguarded.

Well, you decide it is safe to un-guard and have sex. He discovers that the unguarded you is not what he is looking for because he can now see an added dimension to your relationship that he wasn't expecting, e.g., jealousy, demanding and controlling tendencies, among other flaws.

You see, once emotions really get involved after being guarded, most change their personality. In many cases women are not the same cool person of interest. You may call it being vulnerable; men call it being crazy.

As a coach, I've seen this happened so often, but many women never see it coming, never suspect that he is about to bounce. The man is usually called a dog who is only seeking one thing. Here is the question to ask yourself: *Am I the same person he became interested in? Did I change after sex?*

Now let me add the timing issues. Everything I mentioned is in play BUT, you dropped your guard after he decided to move on because he was tired of waiting and feeling like a suspect, even though you may have been kind of fun. Well, here comes the sex based on your decision to un-guard. He will take the sex and see if it can change his mind about his decision. But it doesn't. Maybe he did not enjoy the sex because it was awkward with no passion and he bounced as he had already decided. Can you see how all of this plays out?

The key is to have a consistent personality before and after sex. However the after sex behavior should make you the woman he cannot live without. Not the emotional beast from hell that places all types of pressure on him and is no longer fun to be with.

This is a cycle that so many never understand.

After Sex Behavior

"He just stopped calling after sex. I just feel so cheap."

I just explained your unguarded behavior. Now let me talk more about how your after-sex behavior can cause a man to bounce shortly.

First, let's look at what is really motivating your choices. Then you can learn how to NOT be at the mercy of events.

Women often say that men stop calling directly after sex. Often, I've discovered that it was not totally the truth! Why would a man waste his time going after extremely hard-to-get goodies? Maybe to a sociopath it is a challenge, but not to the majority of men. It is not happening anymore because there are too many women willing to give it up without too much struggle. If a man patiently waits for sex, not calling the next day is simply extremely rare. This statement is based on my challenging those claims directly and investigating what actually occurred. Yes, there are other factors.

The reason I do this as a coach is not to make you feel badly, but to truly figure out what is causing the men in your life to bounce. This requires helping you to see what is happening from a man's point of view.

For example, I had a case where a woman claimed that a guy did not call her the next day, but here is what actually happened.

They had been going out for four weeks and she decided to have sex and she really gave him a night to remember, just as she stated. Well the next day, he did not call her! What happened? Well, she blew up his phone, sent texts all day long, and left a crazy, damaging message at 9:30 pm.

Guess what? He had told her a week before that he would be in training all day until late that evening preparing for a new private-system launch. His company did not allow any employees to have cell phones because they could not be distracted, nor did they want anyone previewing the launch. They catered food as well, so he had no opportunity to call!

He called her around 11 pm while leaving work, but she had turned her phone off because she had an early day at work and had to get up at 4 am; therefore she was asleep. Next, he noticed that she had left messages and listened to them. What a mess! He was extremely surprised.

Well she called him again, early, on her way to work and he answered. She jumped all over him. An argument developed. She called him all types of names and said, "I thought that you would be different. You make me feel soooo cheap."

He could not get a word in and decided to wait until she calmed down. He reminded her about their conversations over the last week regarding his product launch. Her response, "Ah yeah, now I remember."

But this man decided that this is not the woman for him because of her outburst and it became double the trouble because she believed he was just trying to hit it and leave it anyway. It was NOT the case; but you can't tell her anything.

Now here is the question: Could you blame him for not wanting to be with such a volatile woman? All she had to do was wait to see if something had occurred that was out of his control before jumping to a conclusion. She slept with the guy, but could not give him the benefit of the doubt. She could not have a generally approving spirit instead of being skeptical. He did not want this type of woman; so, of course, he bounced.

Again, I say you can't be at the mercy of events. Find out what happened before you blow up. Your imagination could be deceiving you into believing things that are not in play.

What was motivating her choices? Why did she behave this way? No doubt it connects back to some of the things we've been talking about: past relationships, a need for certainty, negative thinking, characterizations, expectations, and unguarded behavior.

To sum up this section: **you must have patience** to wait things out a bit and not jump to conclusion too quickly.

Also, for the record, please understand that when a man is sexually attracted to you, it only makes him want to have sex. Having sex with him does not translate to how he feels about you. It will not make him call you back or feel any different except for how good you are in bed. Sexual attraction is great but you have to captivate him for more.

His Sexual Performance

A man can simply bounce if he feels that he is under-performing in the bedroom. This can be all in his mind, but for some reason, if that belief exists, he will just bounce. It is really a form of protection of his ego to bounce before he thinks his woman will leave. Again, it can be all in his mind.

Men have a certain way they perform in the bedroom as well as having a certain type of erection that they believe provides the best performance. Additionally, they seek a certain type of reaction from a woman when having sex. If a man is not able to reach that type of erection, hear a certain sound or reaction, perform a certain technique, or handle his sexual business as he believes he can, he may question his performance or think that you may feel that he is not hitting it right.

This can bruise his ego tremendously and create all types of mind chatter—explanations or questions about his performances. Signs that this is happening include the "Did you cum?" question. Or, he may say something like, "I normally do this in the bedroom, but…." He is seeking a reaction out of you regarding his performance.

If you are slow to understand where he is coming from and not able to discuss exactly how the sex was for you, his mind will continue wondering about his performance. If you have sex a second time and it's the same way for him, he will just bounce. You may not have a clue; it could be due to his performance.

If you are not the type to be expressive in the bedroom or talk about sex between you and a new lover, just know that these are grounds for a major bounce.

He Is NOT a Jerk, It's Just Biology!

He is so into you and really enjoying the moment. It is building up and he has a massive release, yes he ejaculates. Next he is sleepy and acts as if he does not want to be there. He actually wants to go to sleep and be alone; he may desire to go home. You become upset and feel cheap, thinking he is inconsiderate; that he just came, got what he wanted, and left.

What just happened was a biological event that can be measured. It's called oxytocin and testosterone.

A man needs a high dose of oxytocin in order to ejaculate. After the ejaculation, however, his level rapidly decreases and the letdown makes him feel drained and sluggish. Next his testosterone levels increase and create the feeling of wanting to be alone. He just wants to sleep!

Most women on the other hand still have high levels of oxytocin and will be relaxed and some will sleep. If she is not tired, however, she will also have the feeling of wanting to be close or affectionate. This is because oxytocin is enhanced by her estrogen.

I've noticed that some women who have been extremely hurt or had negative relationship influences growing up will have the exact symptoms as men in this case. However, when checked out medically, they also have low oxytocin levels and other hormonal issues are prevalent.

When you understand the why behind something, it should make it easier to accept. So understand that he is not a jerk, it is something that happens on a chemical level. Don't blame him for something that happens naturally.

Chapter 6

Some Nuances

*"If he says he is okay, believe him. Just because
you are not okay, are feeling uneasy, is not relevant.
He can be silent and happy. So stop asking."*

Infatuation Guilt

Infatuation guilt can explain why a man bounces out of a relationship. It is another biology issue and actually applies to men and women. I believe it is extremely important to include this subject here for your consideration. Infatuation guilt develops when you meet a person and the feelings are off the chain, very explosive: one cannot eat or sleep thinking about that man or woman. But after about two to three months and sex, one or both have lost that loving feeling.

Believe it or not, the reaction can be measured biologically within the brain by its secretion of *Phenyl ethylamine*. Your body actually experiences this exhilarating feeling similar to that of cocaine or ecstasy. Yes, it can be a drug! But do you know why? It's a natural process that is designed to continue the species by reproducing. This is why so many say, "We had amazing chemistry." Although it feels like using drugs, it is a natural high.

What we all should know is that love does not create this type of high within itself. Yes, you can have chemistry with love, but love in itself is a strong connection between two souls.

The purpose of this topic is to help you understand how one can become guilty for having such strong feelings of infatuation in the beginning, but no longer feel the same way later. Many relationships are continued because of guilt or loneliness. Most of us do not want to be alone, so we use the other person to pass the time away until we can find an upgrade in a man or woman.

This is why he/she keeps cheating or talking to other men or women. They are either seeking that feeling again or just trying to find something better. Sorry, but they are seeking to no avail.

I hope you are not disappointed by what I'm about to say. Please understand the truth about all the novels you read and the movies you see that make you feel or say "Aweeee, that's so special!" It is usually not the case! They always show this perpetual high and love at first sight romance in the movies and books.

True love does not work this way at all. Yes, there is a connection at first, but the feeling of love requires time to develop. Also true love usually grows and changes within the relationship. You do not have a steady high like infatuation that always fades eventually and never comes back.

Stop feeling guilty and be straight. Let this person know how you really feel. If you are honest, maybe this can be a person you will grow to love via values and understanding. Stop searching for that feeling. Always evaluate the relationship instead of the person you are with. We always think we can do better and upgrade our current love affairs. The question should be, "Are you doing better in this relationship than ever before?" If you evaluate the person, their skills and education, you may become confused as to whether or not it will work. Instead, you should know how this man makes you feel in the relationship.

Think of a relationship as a three-legged stool: first there is you, second your mate, and third the relationship.

One leg cannot be supported without the others. So the relationship is a leg all by itself and you should judge this more than you are judging your mate.

Again, remove the guilt, be honest, and allow the chips to fall wherever they do. If you are not too attached to the outcome of the relationship, it could be the start of true lasting love. You see, your soul mate could be that man you are looking at right now; but you just don't know it yet. Think about it!

Your World View

One of the biggest mistakes you can make is to attempt to make your man conform to your world view. That view could be "A man should…." And it is totally subjective, based on what you think or, "I expect my man to do this or that because this is the way it should be done."

Newsflash: Men do not like to be around women with overwhelming expectations. Men know that if these expectations are not met, these women will lose their mind and go off. That pressure is one of the main things that will cause him to bounce.

You have to be honest in your assessment of this matter. What ticks you off about your man? When he is performing a task, and it is not being done the way you want, how do you respond? These are indicators that it is all about your worldview. Just know that your man has his own approach to situations, and when you stop making your opinions law; there can be a reconnection or a stronger bond.

The Godly Man Paradigm

You just read "Your World View," illustrating what can happen when you expect a man to conform to yours. This section of the book is designed for my devout religious readers, primarily Christians, who are waiting on God for their mates. Your world view from a religious vantage point is extremely important and must be discussed.

So....You Want a Godly Man? Well your soul mate may be bouncing because you are not clear. As a coach, I'm finding so many Christian single women confused about what they want from a religious perspective. When I have women of faith list their requirements and wants for a mate, I usually get: "I want a Godly man, a man of prayer; we must be equally yoked, etc."

My role as a coach is to ask a client questions and explore with her who each really is as a person. My goal is to take steps to totally understand her and her world, to support and help her find her own answers. I encourage my clients to be extremely clear about what they desire and what vision they have for their life, or what vision they believe God has for their life. Doing this with single, Christian women, is more difficult than I ever imagined.

Why? Well, the key is to make sure that they understand how their thinking from a religious perspective affects their relationship decisions. The goal is to help them understand true character instead of some unauthentic or mystical concepts.

To explain this paradigm, I once had a session with a Christian woman who became a little angry at a few questions about their rules and shouted: "I'll know by the Spirit, if you have the Holy Spirit, you'll just know." Then she said "any person of God will know what I mean about being equally yoked, because all you have to do is follow the word."

I only challenged her response because she was NOT able to answer hardly any of my questions about what she believed. She was over 40, never married, three children with different fathers before salvation, teaches Sunday school and told me that she was seeking a man of God (Godly man). She also said that she was seasoned and ready for God's actions.

Here are the exact questions I asked her. Now see if you can answer them with clarity.

- So, you want a Godly man?
- What is a Godly man?
- What does "to be Godly" mean to you?
- What would a relationship look like, feel like, or be like with this Godly man?
- How would you know that he is Godly?
- Can it be measured from your spiritual perspective?
- Do you actually live your life according to your religious beliefs or doctrines?
- If not, are you seeking this mate to live as you do now?
- Are you seeking this mate to live as you believe you should live because you will correct your behavior later?

- This is important because if yes, will he accept you as you believe now?
- List what you believe it takes to be equally or unequally yoked in a relationship?

You see I've noticed guys bouncing simply because of unclear religious perspectives regarding relationships. Both are believers, but they attend different churches. Now for the record, it is not their beliefs that are different but the "home church" concept is what is keeping them apart. There are many religious cultures but most have the same value system and beliefs on big things; it is usually only one or two minor rules that separate them. This is why so many Christian women are single because they are NOT able to find a suitable mate in their own home church. However, a suitable one is at another church with the same values system on the big things. But these men are rejected all the time. Additionally, a man will bounce because a woman is so stuck on very minor rules that separate them to the point that there are arguments.

I've also found that most of the time, these women do not practice their religious beliefs fully; but because of church peers, they pretend they do.

This is why I urge you to get clear about your true values based on your religious perspective. This will prevent you from rejecting a man in your proximity who has your core beliefs. It is really about matching your words with your true beliefs.

Remember beautiful religious expressions and talk has to be matched with understanding what it means to you. This allows you to know how to make the walk match the talk; especially in your relationship selection. Otherwise, the response you will get from others praising your talk (mainly things you say like "Jesus is my husband and companion)" will be your reward and it could keep you single. Most of the time it does not really translate into getting the mate that God has for you anyway.

My message to you is to get clear about what you truly believe and are actually practicing.

First Date Attire

Men respond on a subconscious level to soft fabrics that will bring out the protector in him. If you appear soft and fragile it's a plus because men are protectors by nature. Business suits and attire can make you appear competitive and physically strong so watch out for that.

Also, please note that men can put you in a category based upon your appearance, especially on your first meeting or date. It doesn't mean that you are like this, but it is his view of the way you look or dress.

This is also the case in online dating based on the picture attached to your profile.

Here are the categories:

1. **Classy:** He will treat you like a lady and be very gentlemanly. He will think that you are the type to take home to his mother or friends. This is where most women want to be, but you must speak, dress, and look the part to be in this category.

2. **Standoffish:** He thinks that you appear to be uppity or arrogant, can't get your hands dirty, and may be difficult to deal with. He will also think that you are expensive.

3. **High Maintenance:** *Can I Afford Her?* This is the question that will be in his head. He thinks that you appear to be all about status, money,

and power. You will be considered financial trouble for most men. Sometimes you are heavy on the makeup. It can also be what you order on the first date.

4. **Over-done:** He thinks that you have too much of everything: makeup, hair extensions or weave, nails. It is over-powering and distracting.

5. **Simple:** He thinks that you dress cute at times but look very simple in most cases. A higher version of Plain Jane.

6. **Plain Jane:** He thinks that you are not very stylish; you are wearing very little or no makeup.

7. **Physical or loose:** The way you look or dress makes him think of sex and this is what he will want to do with you. He will think, *I can make a move on her on tonight and may get it.*

8. **Ghetto or Trashy:** No explanation needed. You know it when you see it.

There is no way around this; you are simply categorized. Please understand that many men will change their minds more often about women who are Standoffish or High Maintenance after a great conversation. You may appear to be in one of those categories upon sight, but can easily persuade him by your attitude that you are really a classy/standard type of lady.

On the first date, just keep it simple and do not dress too sexy. Please don't wear overpowering perfume, too much makeup, or those creative-type nails. I've tested this several times and much of this can place you in the "ghetto/trashy" category simply based on your appearance.

Another test shows that too much makeup can make you appear "high maintenance" and men do not want the hassle. If your make-up is flawless and you are dressed with lady-like tendencies, this is the best choice. Be very classy.

Ladies who do not wear lots of makeup, but put their lipstick on heavily create another issue to which men have an unfavorable response. It's okay to put on your lipstick, but do it lightly, just to add color, and do not make it overpowering. The interesting part about this is you do not look that much different. Lipstick alone does not make you appear more feminine and it is very obvious. Again, use it for a little color; it must be very light to prevent that response.

Men like well-groomed women, including your hair, nails and toes. Try French tip nails and toes, men love this and, for some reason, look at women who wear this differently on the first date. I've tested this several times with hundreds of relationship-worthy men. Also if you are going plain on the hands and toes, this is great too, but be well-groomed. Why? Really, I don't know because men could never explain why they have a different opinion of women regarding their hands and nails. This is weird but works on the first date.

Make sure that you dress properly for the occasion. If the event requires jeans and sneakers, wear that and not dress shoes. I know a lady who wears pumps to bowling alleys when invited. Her response? "This is who I am." Well maybe so, but when meeting a guy on the first date or meeting his family, you do not want to do such a thing.

One more point for your consideration is the smell of your clothes. Ladies, know that what you wear smells like its environment. If your home or closet smells, or has a stale odor, so will your clothes; it will pierce through your perfume. I've heard countless guys speak about a woman whose clothes smell, but not her body. I know that dry cleaning can be expensive, but not having fresh-smelling clothes could prevent you from getting to first base with your dream guy, or he will just bounce.

While we are discussing first dates, make sure you do the following:

- Have eye contact on the date
- Touch him often on the hands and arm gently and smile
- Compliment him especially on his choices and other things
- Tell him how much you are enjoying yourself
- Always say thank you
- Be extremely interested in his conversation.
- No pressure questions; just have fun

Financial Struggles

> **Tip** After the first date the average guy, even a successful one, asks himself, *Can I afford this woman?* If he feels she is too materialistic, he will bounce and not call back. Here is the key: you cannot make suggestions about what to buy until there is a steady relationship. Allow him to offer.

This global economic reset has created huge issues within the dating scene. So much more than you can imagine. We are coming out of it slowly, but have a ways to go. Here is a secret for you: many professionals are struggling too. They have huge student loans and many feel pressure to appear to live at a certain financial standard. For example, they must have the best seats at concerts, an acceptable home in a classy area, or a car that's appropriate to their title.

Those most affected by the economy are men. What does this mean? You have great guys with character struggling financially. How does this affect dating? It is more about how men feel compared to others and most of the time it is about money. Again, no man wants to be around a woman who creates an environment that makes him feel like a failure.

What should you do? You must be concerned about his wallet. Know that he is not a free loader. He has respect. He has character. He is just going through a financial setback and is not able to do some of the things he desires, such as taking you to special restaurants, going out every weekend, going to that concert. Also the higher gas prices could interrupt his frequent visits and outings.

Keep in mind that a man will be silent about his financial situation because he is proud and may be afraid of how you will view him. However some will share this information outright. Become creative when you are dating. Let him know that it doesn't require a lot to have fun. The goal is to spend more time and enjoy each other while growing.

Do not complain about not seeing a man as much if he lives across town and is underemployed. Go see him or meet him in his area if possible. If you are accustomed to men doing all the spending, you may be in for a shock nowadays. This will definitely limit your dating options. Your complaining will run him away (he will bounce) because it will make him feel as if he is not able to make you happy. Thus, he will feel like a failure.

There has to be shared financial responsibility during this time. Those who understand this will win in the end. Because remember, he is the cream of the crop in character and not a free loader, but just a man struggling at this point financially. Just think where your relationship could go with your total support.

Text this man. Tell him how much you appreciate him. Let him know what he does to make you happy. Encourage him. Put a smile on his face. He will get over this situation and will be so thankful he had you.

Grown Son Living at Home

Another big reason why men bounce is when a woman has her grown son living at home. Bringing another man into the house usually causes testosterone clashes and disruptive problems in the house. The woman is placed in a position of not being able to have the love of her life while also pleasing her son.

What I've noticed in my research is that women with a grown son(s) living at home are not able to secure a new relationship-worthy man, especially if that son is not doing anything with his life or has a troubled history. Don't get me wrong, you can get a man, but most of the time he may not fit your standards.

What I am saying is that more good relationships have dissolved because of this situation than almost anything else; it is at least a top-ten problem. It has always been a deal-breaker. Men in my research have always had a problem with this matter and usually will not marry a woman in this situation. Many times, he will take the goodies or a cookie from time to time, but never develops a lasting relationship as long as there are grown children, especially men, living with her.

Did you see the movie *Baby Boy*? Well, it really shows some of the conflicts but it had a successful ending. My research shows a different result, i.e., ending unsuccessfully. Yes, there are some that have a great ending, but just like *Baby Boy*, the grown son had to go.

Here are my questions:

1. If you want a man in your life, how will you deal with your grown son?
2. Why is your grown son living with you anyway? Also, do you allow him to call the shots? Is he troubled?
3. What role do you want a new mate to have in your home with your grown son?
4. Do you make excuses for your son as to why he is getting into trouble, not working, or not contributing?
5. Is he going to school and contributing in other ways?

Ladies, the only thing I can say is that in my research men just did not like this matter. This is why so many women with a grown son living at home have difficulties keeping that relationship-worthy man around.

> **Tip** **Your children, especially grown sons could be a huge reason why a man may bounce.** Simply because they could clash. Blending a family is extremely hard. Getting clarity on this issue early is a plus.

Moms with Young Children

First never see or think that having children and being single is baggage. It is NOT! I know there are men who actually seek a woman with children and it could be motivated by many reasons. Some men love motherhood and find it sexy, some men understand that he will have more freedom because she has other responsibilities, or he may not be able to have kids on his own. A single moms may not have men coming in and out of her life and may be more trusting if he's been hurt before. Whatever the reason, just know that if it works for him and his lifestyle, he will want a single mom.

On the other hand, if you are a mom with young children there can be issues and some men will bounce. Many will never explain why, but I've listed the reasons here. First, let me say that I have two names for these types of moms. You can be a **single mom** or a **solo mom**. What's the difference? Well, a single mom will have the child's father in their lives, while a solo mom does not. He could be deadbeat, estranged, or maybe dead. Yes, it can make a difference to a man what type of mom category you fit into and how big of a headache he will encounter.

Here are ten (10) reasons men bounce from women with children.

1. **"I Can't Find a Babysitter"**: Women will use this as an excuse to get out of a date with a man, or they may legitimately not be able to

find a babysitter. In either case, it isn't the man's problem and you shouldn't ask him to deal with it.

2. **Baby's Daddy:** When a man is dealing with a woman and getting to know her, he shouldn't have to deal with the baby's father. Some guys can't get over the fact that their ex has moved on. Before he was an inattentive jerk and didn't give a damn about her. Now that another man has entered the picture, the dude wants to be the ideal boyfriend and a "father of the year" nominee. The guy starts stalking her and wants to fight the new boyfriend. Even if the woman and her ex are on good terms, the guy feels as if he can always smash. He knows her. He knows what she wants to hear and what makes her happy. The next thing you know you are having this conversation: "I've decided to try and make it work with the baby's dad." Therefore, some men feel that the best way to avoid this situation is to avoid single moms.

3. **Rent-a-Daddy:** Can you be a father to my son? Women with children are often searching for a role model for their sons. This is OK. A good guy will be into that. Do you just want a guy because of your son or daughter?

4. **The Kids Are Still Up:** Men understand that a woman does not want to bring her man around her kids too fast, but there are times when she

is not able to leave and come to his place. This is when he will come over. However, she is not good at managing her kid's bedtime, and they are still up. Guys bounce because of this all the time.

5. **You're Not My Dad:** A man starts seeing a woman seriously. He notices that her children have behavior issues, throwing or breaking things and not being very respectful of adults. If he sees one of the kids doing something dangerous and attempts to protect him, a resentful child will shout "You can't tell me what to do! You're not my dad!" A guy will bounce if you are not able to manage your children.

6. **Trying To Get Pregnant:** Some men believe women will meet a successful new guy in an attempt to get pregnant to pay for other children. Sad but true in many cases. He will bounce if you come on strong or too fast in the sex area.

7. **Bad Judge of Character:** If a woman got knocked up by a grossly irresponsible guy who has been this all of his life, the new man in her life will bounce because he can see that she is a bad judge of character and he knows there could be issues in the future. He would rather that the father be irresponsible in the area of

relationships than in life (the ability to earn a living).

8. **Unnecessary Expenditures:** Eventually you'll get to meet the kid(s). Soon those dates turn into family outings. Instead of paying for two people, you're paying for three or more. He will bounce when this happens too fast.

9. **Tag, You're It!** This should be the biggest deterrent to ever dealing with a single mother. In some jurisdictions, I think California is one of them, if you start dealing with a female with kids, move in with her, and things go south, the female can sue you for child support. Imagine that! She can claim that she and the child have "become accustomed to your supporting the child." You could end up possibly paying child support for a kid that isn't even yours. Imagine being extorted money because you were doing what you thought was the "right thing"! The state doesn't give a rat's ass about the relationship being over or your being a "good guy." They just don't want the chick on welfare. So as far as you're concerned, it's "Tag, you're it!"

10. **Baby Damage:** Women who do not take care of themselves after birth. Some guys call this "birth trauma." Pregnancy leaves stretch marks, saggy breasts, and c-section scars. Sometimes the vagina is stretched out. Guys

understand this, but they have to notice her making an effort to take care of herself, or they will bounce. **NOTE:** most of the time, its younger guys or guys into major fitness who may consider this an issue.

Girlfriend Peer Pressure

There is no doubt or denying the strength of women.

Women are asked to be everything to everyone, but at the same time face pressure from within their own sisterhood. Pressure to obtain it all: fashionable clothes, big house, luxury cars, great man with status, and the whole world.

It has been said that many women walk around depressed and do not know it; there are books on this subject.

Girlfriend peer pressure (the stress that women put on each other) contributes greatly to the stress women feel and the stress they can place on a man. This is another reason why he bounced.

Another example of pressure can be if a girlfriend asks questions in front of your man regarding what he purchased for you on your birthday or a special occasion. After your response, she will make facial expressions as if it was not enough. If you don't correct her promptly, that's a sure way to make a man bounce. Example: "So, he bought you that watch, what else did he purchase with it? What about some earrings or a trip, is that all you got was that watch?"

If you don't fix that directly, watch him bounce unless you made him aware of this person's behavior beforehand. Don't allow you girlfriends to put uncomfortable pressure on you or your man.

Jealous Friends

The information to follow about jealous friends could make the difference between either obtaining that magical relationship or not, and why he bounced. First I want to start off by giving you a quick story.

TC met this nice lady Niecy who was attractive, but somewhat of a plain Jodie—although it didn't matter to him because he loved her mind and sincerity. He asked her out for lunch one day. It was a very nice date, and they both decided to see each other again.

The next date was a dressy-casual function and he got a chance to meet all of Niecy's girlfriends, a few family members, and many of her associates. Guess what? She changed right before his eyes. He was wondering what happened to this sincere woman who had piqued his interest.

Unbeknownst to him, a pack of four girlfriends, and two female family members were asking her questions about him because he was so much higher in status than guys she had gone out with before, and better than the guys with her friends. What was his type? The corporate look with clean-cut style. Her friends were teasing hard while suggesting that he was probably a playboy looking to score that night. They spoke as if she did not deserve him and would be taken advantage of. One friend actually thought that he was from an escort service and was paid to be with her. WOW, with friends like this who needs enemies?

TC noticed that Niecy started to make all types of demands of him and began asking crazy questions. She said things like, "Go get this for me. I need this. Aren't you going to do this or that? Are you a playboy?" and "What do you want from me?"

It took him aback at first, but he realized what was happening. He pulled her aside and said, "What is the problem here?" Niecy said that she received feedback from her friends. They thought that TC was nice, but not her type and that she would get hurt dealing with him. He asked her what she felt when they were out before and speaking on the phone and she replied, "Well, very special; and it was sooooo exciting."

So, Ladies, can you see what happened here? We had two people very interested in each other, and it all ended because of peers. She needed the approval of her friends, and it was over just like that.

Just think about this: She wanted an attentive, clean-cut style guy. She met a clean-cut style guy! But then she wanted the approval of her friends. Ladies, this may never happen.

You see, your friends and some family members may say they want the best for you, but if you bring home a guy that they think is better in any way than what they currently have or don't have, it is possible that they will get jealous and attempt to sabotage your relationship.

Now let's talk about what TC was doing compared to her friends' men. By the way, three did not have one; the others had dates. TC was very attentive. He pulled her chair out for her, stood when she was leaving, took off her coat, asked if she would like a drink--things that good guys (relationship-worthy guys) do and say.

In contrast, the men with those ladies who criticized TC were not attentive at all. They were not very gentlemanly and really did not like TC standing when his date left. One said to him, "Hey, man, it's 50/50 nowadays."

TC told them that he was from the old school and treated women with respect; he continued being very attentive to Niecy and did not apologize for this. Yes, he spoke to the men in a very respectable manner and with a smile. One guy said, "I hear you" and started being more attentive to his date.

Now, note this: the friends who were the most aggressive to Niecy about TC did not have a date.

I can also tell you several stories regarding women who are very opinionated about men. They always make references to what they want or should get from a man instead of trying to be a good mate. This is why most do not have a man and are always hanging around other women without men. You see, misery loves company.

When I share this story with women they often say "I know females who are like this, but they are not ones I hang out with." Here is my question: "Are you sure?"

My goal is to help you meet and keep relationship-worthy men, not jerks. Most women get jerks all the time. If you want a real relationship-type man, your friends, and—yes—family, may not support you if they do not have the same. It is time to make a choice: him vs. them. You will still love them and hang out, but girl, get your man!

As for Niecy, the lady I mentioned earlier, she is still searching for the right guy, seeking approval from her friends and family. It has been over two years. I told her that sometimes friends and family can keep you from being happy. Guess what she said to me? "Not the ones I hang out with." (A true story)

What is it going to be: him or them? This is why he bounced.

Final Remarks

You just read what a huge sampling of men have said about why they bounced from a relationship.

- Yes, there are exceptions. My goal was to give you a glimpse into the minds of men.
- Yes, some may believe this is too much for women to handle.
- Just remember, good treatment of your man is by his standards not yours.

Here is something to consider. My goal is to help you feel safe enough in your relationship to become vulnerable because, without this, a man will bounce. This is the key to a lasting relationship: the willingness to be vulnerable. And remember, those in a relationship are allies not opponents.

He will not want to waste his time being blamed for your past and will move on fast. What you fear the most is actually the only way to find true love. Women ask me all the time "When is it safe to let down my guards?" My response has always been the same: When he says that you are exclusive, it is time. Just keep in mind that being too guarded can hurt extremely in the getting-to-know-you process. It's okay to be cautious, but also be fun and loving. Just remember that an unguarded you may not be to his liking either. Just remain consistent, but better, once you drop your guard.

I hope you are able to establish a great relationship and would love to hear your comments and feedback. If you are looking for personal coaching, I would love to assist in helping you create the love you deserve. Just go to the website: www.philturnerjr.com

50 Quick Tips

A quick review of tips from the book plus more

1st.   **"Whatever!"** Feeling frustrated? Not
       understanding? That's a red flag for gender-
       reasoning differences. Alert! Your "Whatever!"
       attitude will usually drive him away.

2nd.   **Gender differences?** *What is a man's perfect day
       (compared to mine?)* Sex? Blowjob? More sex?
       What about taking a big dump, winning at
       anything, playing or watching great sports, being
       left alone, getting a great night's sleep. These are
       primal instincts; they only require your
       understanding, not a roll of the eyes and a
       "Whatever!"

3rd.   **A man pursues a loving relationship and
       connection through sex** and discovers the
       woman he cannot live without after great sex.
       BUT sexual attraction can be just that and
       nothing more. You have to captivate him for
       more.

4th.   A constant smile, being authentic, having self-
       confidence with sensuality plus a strong
       approving attitude towards all men, is an
       attraction magnet.

5th. **You cannot ask a guy to make a life-time decision on you in a short period of time.** This is not happening. It will not work. Therefore, you must know how you personally react after sex before you take that step. Your reactions will make the difference.

6th. **If you are looking for a highly successful or educated man, know that he is looking for intellect**--a woman who can handle her own business, and has a plan. Being fine, cute, and sexy is not cutting it anymore. If you don't bring anything else to the table, he will not see a future with you. You have to be smart and moving towards your goals.

7th. **A man can bounce for reasons that some may believe are insane, but they can be real to him.** When a man asks you not to do or wear something, pay attention. It could be triggering a **global belief** he has from the past. If something you do or wear matches that belief, **he may bounce.**

8th. **Never assume that a man's character is based on the guys he associates with or hangs around.** He can still be totally true to his woman and a great guy. **Get to know him before you judge.**

9th. **A man wants to feel good in your presence.** He wants to be <u>acknowledged</u>, <u>respected</u>, <u>trusted</u>, <u>appreciated,</u> and made to feel that he is your personal <u>superman</u>. The things you do determine his emotional calculation of these factors. If the mental math doesn't add up, he will bounce.

10th. **"I trust you" is one of the most powerful things you can say to a guy.** He will want to live up to that brand.

11th. **Men try to see things better than they are because they are wired for victory.** Testosterone is biological fuel for winning and solving problems.

12th. **Do not judge his intentions, especially if he does not see a point that is obvious to you.** Men do the best they can and deserve to receive a sense of good-will attitude from you.

13th. **A man's dating skills do not translate into what type of husband he will be for you.**

14th. If you take what you are looking for into consideration, **what does the male pool look like for you?** How many men out there will fit your criteria?

15th. **Very good-looking men have many, many options.**

16th. **A man who is seriously looking will not want competition. Date other men while seeing him; most will bounce.** This was a 10-to-1 type of response in my survey of men.

17th. **Men don't think about what you are NOT, it is about what you ARE to them.** *"My arms are too big, My butt is getting fat, My hair is not right."* This is your negative thinking; not the man's. He does not evaluate you as you do yourself.

18th. So many women say, "I'm a lady and you are not supposed to show interest before he does." Well if you don't, he will bounce. **Don't play games.**

19th. **Remember: Whatever you focus on with a man is how he grows in the relationship.** If the focus is negative or name calling, he will grow in negativity; if it is positive, he will grow in a positive manner.

20th. **"Listen to me! Are you listening?" Men have a tendency to tune out frequently while in a conversation with a woman.** This is not intentional. **Biologically he is wired to fix things and has a need for you to get to the point.**

21st. **Don't quote relationship rules to him.** Men wonder, *Who made up these relationship rules?* Just watch to see if these rules help or hinder your developing a great relationship.

22nd.   **Never make fun of your man in public**—about anything! Not his hair, clothes, shoes, or any mistake he makes. Don't buy into others teasing him, either. Stand by your man!

23rd.   **Never describe an ex or acquaintance to a man of interest or he will bounce.** He can see for himself how they look.

24th.   It is not about how good you look, how good the sex is, how religious you are, or anything you may think that keeps your man with you. **It is about the way you make him feel, period.**

25th.   **What is not good to one man can be absolutely wonderful to another.** Just stop thinking that it is good to ALL.

26th.   **A man needs and wants you to reach an orgasm,** bust a nut, or to cum (whatever phrase you like to use). He understands that there will be times that you will not, but this has to be the exception.

27th.   **Lack of sexual spontaneity is frustrating to men.** You have to be able to sneak a quickie to take the edge off your man from time to time, or he will bounce.

28th. **Make sure you truly know that he is interested in you before sex.** Get to know him first, without allowing a passionate build up. When he presses, gently let him know you have standards, Say, *"I know you are turned on and I want to give you a night to remember, but I only have sex with my boyfriend."* This is not pressuring a man for a life-time commitment.

29th. **Asking questions is great and necessary, but it cannot be excessive or it feels like a job instead of a relationship.** Relax and see if you can enjoy his company; watch and listen and feel.

30th. **Your children, especially grown sons could be a huge reason why a man may bounce.** Simply because they could clash. Getting clarity on this issue early is a plus.

31st. **Blending a family is extremely difficult.** Don't expect him to play by the rules that you and your ex established. He is the man of his house and his rules are applicable.

32nd. **When a guy makes claims about the future with you, make sure you match these words with actions.** What is the follow-up response to his words? You may just be Ms. Right Now instead of Mrs. Future. **The key is** to be cautious and watch out for predators. They are around and look for desperate women.

33rd. **After the first date the average guy, even a successful one, asks himself,** *Can I afford this woman?* If he feels she is materialistic, he will bounce and not call back. **Here is the key:** you cannot make suggestions about what to buy until there is a steady relationship. Allow him to offer.

34th. **A man only wants to make you happy and is very discouraged when he cannot.** An unhappy woman means that he has failed as a man. Make it extremely clear how he can be successful in making you happy; and keep it simple.

35th. **Most men don't like aggressive women.** It takes away the hunt. (Men who tolerate your aggression may be seeking to take something from you.) When you feel like pursuing an attractive man, it's your dopamine and testosterone levels increasing. Learn to tame your primal instincts, your body chemistry.

36th. **He is not your girlfriend.** Don't expect him to act like one; he is not wired that way. Yes, he can listen, solve problems, and cuddle if necessary. He connects totally when he can be absolutely himself.

37th. **Men do not interpret things or communicate the same way as women.** That's why they **complement one another.** His brain is not wired (as yours is) to connect the dots between now and the past. To him this issue is about this moment.

38th. **If he says he is okay, believe him.** Just because you are not okay, are feeling uneasy, is not relevant. He can be silent and happy. So stop asking.

39th. It is **not true** that if a man loves you enough he will change his mind, especially regarding **children.** If he says he doesn't want them, believe it. If you must have them, move on ASAP.

40th. Just because a man wears sun glasses at night or wears unfashionable clothing does not represent what his character will be in a relationship with you. **Some great guys have a great woman to clean them up a bit without changing who he is.**

41st. **You can never change a man**; it is just that simple. **He can only grow being with you.**

42nd. **If you snoop he will bounce!** When he catches you checking his phone, his computer files, his emails, his Facebook or Twitter accounts, or anything like this, he will bounce. If you persuade him to stay, he will NEVER see you the same, especially if he has nothing to hide. **If you don't trust him, why should be trust you?**

43rd. **Guys who do dumb things can still make great mates,** but your indignant reaction can make it impossible for you to find out. **Plan for such scenarios. First,** always think before you act. Go back and review the book. Call me. **Second,** ascertain if he actually really loves and wants you. **Third,** follow your plan.

44th. **Never tell a love interest how much another guy has spent on you.** He will bounce if you do. What another guy purchased for you is no-one else's business. Keep it that way.

45th. **Never test a man's faithfulness using a friend** or other tactics. If he finds out, he will bounce.

46th. **Establish boundaries, but don't bitch.** Men bounce from bitches every day. But don't be so nice that you allow others to take advantage of your kindness.

47th. **Men do not marry because they love you; they only marry when they are simply ready.** Never think his love will change this. You can attempt to force his hands, but he will become resentful and bounce.

48th.   **Men instinctively conceal their intentions because they are hunters and warriors.** They are not attempting to be secretive or to lie; they just don't want to show their hand. If a warrior shows an aggressor his hand, he will not survive. You must understand this dynamic and stop believing that men just lie.

49th.   A man usually manipulates and schemes to get sex and attention from a woman; however, women manipulate and scheme to get men to commit. **Both are manipulative** to get what they need the most from each other.

50th.   **You may see** yourself as an "I know what I want," accomplished, witty, very conversational type of person with ambitious ways. **He may see** you as arrogant, bossy, competitive, argumentative, and extremely difficult to deal with. **He is seeking** a mate to complement him and fit into his life, NOT a business partner.

19722242R00123

Made in the USA
Lexington, KY
03 January 2013